BONE BROTH BENEFITS & EASY BONE BROTH RECIPES

HOW TO MAKE BONE BROTH FOR ANTI-AGING, BEAUTY, HEALING, AND SEXY BODY-SLIMMING

K. SUZANNE

Green
Butterfly
Press

ABOUT THE AUTHOR

Kristen Suzanne is an author traveling the world with her family on a multi-year odyssey to experience other cultures and stay fit while she stuffs her face with their food. (For now, meat anyway.)

See Kristen's blog at:

GlobalKristen.com

Twitter: @KristensRaw

Instagram: global_kristen

CONTENTS

OTHER BOOKS BY K. SUZANNE

The Carnivore Diet Handbook

The Frugal Carnivore Diet

Carnivore Diet Intermittent Fasting

Sardine Solution

Recipes with Sardines

INTRODUCTION

For a free, printable .PDF "Bone Broth Cheat Sheet" (which includes the recipes in this book), email me at kristen@globalkristen.com.

I was drawn to bone broth, a centuries-old, universal "superfood" because it seemed so mysterious.

I'm usually adventurous when it comes to diet and food. In fact, I always enjoyed the shock value I'd get telling people I was doing X or eating Y. Going vegan, and then raw vegan, did that for awhile... and it seemed to be an overall healthy choice. That is, until my family became depleted and ill from eating vegan. That's a story for another time. I'm now firmly on the other side of the diet spectrum and eating a carnivore diet, which has been a fascinating health journey. You can read all about it in my book, The Carnivore Diet Handbook.

After I pulled my vegan head out of my ass, and before I went carnivore, the magic of bone broth came onto my radar. As I eased out of veganism and started considering animal foods, I did a lot of research on many foods, and bone broth landed on the short list.

I was strangely drawn to bone broth. It seemed almost mysterious. It was attractive because it sounded cool. At that time, bone broth wasn't all the rage like it is now. So, shock-value-enjoyment to be had, when I told people I was going to make bone broth, they looked at me like I had two heads. Wicked fun. It's not a stretch to say that I had visions of myself as a witch, standing over a cauldron of boiling bones, stirring a magical elixir or Potion of Healing.

Flavor Flavor Flavor

I was originally drawn to bone broth because of its nutrition and ancient coolness. But as time went on, I actually found myself continuously using it for culinary reasons. "Stock," as most chefs call bone broth, adds a flavor to recipes that is beyond amazing. Once I started doing really cooking with bone broth, it was impossible to go back to using water in recipes. There was no going back. I was hooked.

Bone broth made all of my food taste so much better. My family just couldn't get enough of my meals whenever I used bone broth to prepare them! I used it in stews, soups, gravies, and sauces for many different meals. I cooked rice and pasta with it. I braised vegetables in it. It makes such a difference in depth of flavor, comfort, and not to mention nourishment, that my kitchen is never without it.

It's Really Just Stock!

The admittedly boring truth about bone broth is that it's simply just good ol' stock. You know, like chicken stock, beef stock, or fish stock. That box (or can) of chicken stock you grab to make gravy? That's bone broth - a name that sounds weightier with promise than "stock." So, while chef's will always say "stock," (or the French "bouillon") I call it bone broth. I suppose there is one tiny difference between stock and bone broth, and that's that chefs tend to not cook it quite as long. That's splitting hairs though. Hardcore bone broth enthusiasts may choose to err on the side of cooking it longer in hopes of extracting a bit more nutrition. So, while a chef might cook chicken bone broth for 4 to 6 hours out of convenience, a home cook might cook it for 12 to 24 hours. There's no hard science to this. Just start cooking some bones and water and enjoy all the benefits to be had: amazing flavor and nutrition.

The Foundation of Cooking

In culinary circles, bone broth is considered the foundation of cooking, and for good reason. A cup of bone broth seems so simple, and for the most part it is. But it can be used in so many wonderful ways. Bone broth really sets the foundational flavor and stage for many recipes.

Michael Ruhlman writes about making stock,

> "It may be the most commonly avoided preparation in America's kitchens, even though it's the single preparation that might elevate a home cook's food from decent to spectacular."

He also says,

> "If there's one preparation that separates a great home cook's food from a good home cook's food, it's stock."

Bone Broth Goes Mainstream

More chefs are using the words "bone broth" these days. That's because bone broth isn't such a weird term anymore. There are restaurants that sell bone broth by the cup for take-out, making it like grabbing a coffee to-go, except it's bone broth to-go. I still giggle thinking about that for some reason. And there are companies from obscure and new to common and reputed who are now using "bone broth" on the labels of their containers instead of "stock." In certain parts of the USA (like Los Angeles, of course), you can even have bone broth delivered to you. Keep that in mind next time you get sick, and don't have any on hand. My mom thinks the next thing on the map will be a Bone Broth Food Truck. (Any takers out there? This could be awesome!)

The point is that bone broth and stock are the same thing. Use whichever term you like. I'll be calling it bone broth in this book. It's been around forever, probably since at least the invention of clay pottery 20,000 years ago, to home kitchens, to modern, trendy restaurants.

In the most simplest terms, bone broth is a liquid food in which bones (chicken, turkey, duck, beef, veal, lamb, pork, or fish) are boiled in water for anywhere from 30 minutes to 48 hours. (This variation in timing depends on the type of bones used, as we'll discuss in Chapter 6.) The bones are then removed and the remaining liquid is consumed. That's it. Bones, water, heat. Simple! In this book, I'll show you how easy and wonderful bone broth is to prepare.

Bone Broth Is Easy to Make

When I started the bone broth journey, I had no idea where to begin, but I quickly learned. It's my hope to introduce bone broth into your home, with excitement, because making bone broth is fun and easy. With a few simple tips, you'll be on your way fast and your life will change with this new staple food.

There are many ways to make bone broth, so no matter the kitchen equipment, I expect you can dive right in. At a most basic level, all you require is a soup pot. A proper "stock pot" is designed better (it's taller than it is wide), but if you don't have one of those, no worries, as a soup pot works fine. I'll also share common ways of making bone broth with a pressure cooker (my favorite is the electric pressure cooker, Instant Pot), or you can use a slow cooker (the most common technique for bone broth lovers). Or the ultimate – you can get fancy and use a Sous Vide Supreme (water oven) to make your bone broth.

Furthermore, making bone broth can be as diversified as the contents in your refrigerator. The sky is the limit. Between the variety of ingredients you can use, as well as use different cooking methods, you'll find many ways to have more bone broth in your life.

Let's get started!

PART I

WHY BONE BROTH?

Chapter 1

THE MAGIC OF BONE BROTH

Bone Broth Primer

Bone broth advocate Dr. J. Axe says, "Bone broth or stock was a way our ancestors made use of every part of an animal. Bones and marrow, skin and feet, tendons and ligaments that you can't eat directly can be boiled and then simmered over a period of days. This simmering causes the bones and ligaments to release healing compounds like collagen, proline, glycine, and glutamine that have the power to transform your health."

What if you could drink something that will help you lose weight, fight inflammation, and improve your overall health? Imagine if you could do that by simply drinking this tasty magical elixir on a regular basis? Something you'd enjoy and look forward to, just like you do a daily cup of coffee or tea? Bone broth is basically that. It's affordable, healing, waist-slimming, and tested, tried-and-true soul-food that you drink. When you drink it regularly, it can be life-changing.

Bone Broth Is Old News.

Bone broth as been around for a long time. Various cultures have used it as a medical treatment for thousands of years. Around the world, bone broth is revered as one of the world's most powerful healing foods. That's a long time, with a reach that is far and wide. It's also a way to stretch your dollar. By cooking the bones that come with your meat, you're able to make more food and meals from the animal.

Bone Broth Minerals

Bone broth has vitamins and minerals like phosphorous, sodium, potassium, and magnesium, to name just a few. It's an easy-to-love drink, with warm savory flavors and salty satisfying goodness. Instead of reaching for that second or third cup of coffee in a day, you could instead choose a delicious drink that actually infuses you with anti-aging, anti-inflammatory, teeth-hair-nails-and-bone-building healing elements.

Bone Broth Collagen

Bone broth is also a source of collagen (that's a protein), which helps the outside of your body look as good as the inside of your body. People anecdotally report bone broth's collagen as improving the appearance of their skin and helping reduce cellulite (which comes from a lack of connective tissue). Bone broth can increase collagen, which could increase connective tissue. This explains why many people believe bone broth helps reduce wrinkles, prevent stretch-marks, and banish cellulite.

Studies also indicate that collagen can help heal the lining of the digestive tract. It also supports the joints, tendons, and bones. Bone broth is the gift that keeps on giving. For some of these benefits, the challenge for most people is getting enough collagen into their diet, unless they're regularly eating cuts of meat that are rich in it. That's where bone broth comes in. It's a great beauty hack when it comes to getting more collagen. Bone broth is your easy way to get a daily delicious dose of skin-tightening, hair-strengthening, digestive-calming, and joint-healing collagen.

Bone Broth Glycine, Arginine, Proline, and Glutamine

It doesn't stop there though. Bone broth is a source of glycine (an amino acid), which has been shown to help people sleep better, improve brain health (memory), detoxify the body, and fight inflammation. It also has arginine, which can regenerate damaged liver cells and produce sperm (to help fertility) and growth hormones. Plus, it contains proline, which is believed to repair a leaky gut, increase metabolism, regenerate cartilage and heal joints. And then there's the glutamine in bone broth, which may help heal the gut lining, facilitate muscle building, and strengthen cells in the small intestine.

Lastly, bone broth is highly reputed for preventing infection. Moms and grandmas routinely serve chicken soup when we're sick (made with anti-viral bone broth, though they might not have realized it). There are studies showing that infections caused by cold and flu viruses can be decreased by drinking chicken broth.

Bone Broth Controversy

So, it would seem that bone broth is the "bees knees" and everyone should drink it. However, not everyone is jumping on the bone broth train. It's true that the field of nutrition is imperfect. So, nutritionists don't agree about the health claims made for bone broth. But just look around to the various cultures all over the world, and study some history. Bone broth has been used for ages, and it's been used for healing! I tend to side with multi-generational use of things, or at least I lean in that direction. Even athletes like Los Angeles Laker Kobe Bryant show love for bone broth. He told the press, "I've been doing the bone broth for a while now. It's great — energy, inflammation. It's great."

Here's the thing. Bone broth definitely has some nutrition. I can see bone broth being effective for health in three camps of people:

1. The bad eaters: Bone broth is helpful for someone eating a conventional, nutrient-poor diet. The bone broth provides a nice supply of missing nutrients.
2. The good eaters: Some people drawn to bone broth are likely to fall into the health-conscious category already. Therefore, by choosing something regularly that's healthy, it automatically means not choosing something that's less healthy. The bone broth displaces potentially bad food choices.
3. The all-star broth consumers: Bone broth is helpful for people drinking it daily, sometimes twice a day or more. This means that there's a steady supply of the nutrients listed above and they are in a quantity to make a difference in health when it's consumed regularly.

So while I don't think bone broth is a complete cure-all for people with bad eating habits (and resulting diseases), I do believe its use as a supplement to a healthy diet can do serious wonders. It has valuable nutrients that, combined with an overall anti-inflammatory diet, could tighten your skin, heal your gut, and strengthen your body overall.

There's no doubt that science is recognizing the power of a healthy digestive system even if they don't yet name bone broth as a way to make it happen. And, any bone broth evangelist will tell you it's one of the keys to them looking and feeling younger than ever.

So, try it. Give it a good go by drinking it regularly, for 2-3 months, to see if you experience the full range of reported benefits. A cup of bone broth just here and there, while a bit helpful, isn't the formula.

Bone broth needs to be a habit. If you're going to glean all the wonderful benefits bone broth can offer, then you need to drink up!

I have to say, though... best of all, in my foodie opinion, bone broth is friggin' delicious. Seriously yummy stuff. Drinking a mug of bone broth makes you feel like you're getting a great big hug and your belly is satisfied with the rich flavors. Once you start making bone broth, you'll not only drink it by the mug regularly, but you'll use it consistently in much of your cooking. Life, and your food, will never be the same.

Bone Broth Taste

Even though humans have been making bone broth since the beginning of time, sadly, most Americans still buy "stock in a box." It's not the same. For starters, the nutrition probably won't be as rich. Second, the flavor doesn't compare. I suspect people never dreamed of making their own bone broth because they just don't know how easy it is to make. But you should make it. Bone broth is nourishing comfort food that tastes delicious on its own, and makes everything you cook with it... sublime.

It's simply a matter of learning a few quick pointers, and bone broth is one of the most forgiving recipes in the world. You really can't muck it up. As mentioned before, there are many different ways to make it based on the type of equipment you use. I have a slow cooker, stock pot, Dutch oven, Sous Vide Supreme, and Instant Pot pressure cooker for making bone broth. I use one of those to make bone broth once or twice a week, so that I'll always have bone broth on hand.

Bone Broth Aroma

The smell of bone broth alone is healing, to me anyway. It calms my soul (reducing stress) when my home is filled with those scents wafting through the air. I especially love waking up in the morning, after it's been cooking all night in the slow cooker. I open my bedroom door to the intense aroma of comfort and I smile. My husband loves coming home to the smell of bone broth cooking. He walks through the door and the first thing he says, "Mmmmm that smells GOOD!"

Enhancing Meals with Bone Broth

My whole family loves bone broth. I get rave reviews, especially on meals where I've used it in place of water. I'll never forget one potluck where I made a great big chuck roast. It was such a crowd-pleaser! I cooked it in bone broth using my Instant Pot pressure cooker. The liquid becomes double-powered in flavor because the broth alone is delicious, but meat cooking in broth adds more meaty-good-flavor on top of that!

So, yes, it's beyond amazing when you use it to make a roast. But I don't stop there. I routinely use it to make recipes like chilis, stews, soups, sauces, gravies, and mashes by using bone broth in place of any water the recipe calls for. I'll make mashed potatoes and when I'm mashing in the heavy whipping cream, I'll mash in a 1/4 to 1/2 cup of bone broth and some accompanying bone broth fat. Or, I'll mash the potatoes with heavy whipping cream and butter and then drizzle on some hot bone broth as a light sauce.

One of my favorite uses of bone broth is making white rice with it instead of water, when cooking. Then, I top the cooked rice with lots of butter and some sea salt. I also make pasta with it in my Instant Pot (see recipe, Bone Broth Pasta in chapter 8). Holy sh*t that makes the most amazing meal. My daughter requests it regularly.

If you're interested in eating greens, but you're not happy about their bitterness, try braising your greens in some reduced bone broth. That's consistently a favored way to consume more greens. The next time you cook your kale, simmer or braise the bunch in some thickened/reduced bone broth. Transfer the mixture to a bowl with the saucy broth along with it. Top it with a squeeze of fresh orange juice and freshly ground black pepper. Wow! Kale will never be the same. (You can also cook kale and broth in the Instant Pot - see Buttered Kale 'n' Broth recipe, chapter 8.)

The brilliant thing is that bone broth enhances the flavor of your recipe so much that you'll think you're sitting in a Michelin Star restaurant. Whether you're saucing up a steak or making a simple soup, everything is deepened in a deliciously intense and comforting way. You'll find yourself speechless while eating.

Taking Bone Broth With Me and Sharing It

When I travel to my mom's house for a few nights, I take a couple quarts of glass mason jars full of bone broth from my freezer. This makes for an easy, hearty breakfast if I'm not in the mood to make eggs or beef. It also means having a cuppa broth at the end of the night, after a meal. While others might opt for sugary-inflammatory desserts, I'm lovingly sipping my salty broth and feeling beyond satisfied.

When I travel with broth to my mom's, I'll sometimes surprise her while she's watching her favorite TV show with a little cup of it. The first time I treated her to this she exclaimed after a few minutes, "What the hell? You gave me this little cup? I want more!" She has such a loving way with words - haha. The bottom line is that I've yet to serve a mug of the delicious elixir to anyone and have it turned down. It's just too damn tasty.

Furthermore, I feel so good sharing this with others. Making bone broth comes from the heart, whether it's your first batch or your hundredth. There's something that's been passed down through our DNA that seems to turn on when making broth from bones and water. It's like we've evolved having consumed this elixir for millennia. When drinking a sip, the body seems to know instinctively that it's good and important. Sharing this feeling with others only makes it that much better.

Chapter 2

HEALING BONE BROTH

Bone broth's reputation is vast and people report benefits such as:

- Helping with food allergies
- Improving digestion
- Eliminating (or greatly reducing) joint pain
- Recovering faster from colds and flu viruses
- Helping you be your most beautiful self with anti-aging properties.

People drink bone broth to increase strength and vitality and fortify the body's reserves while healing from sickness. Bone broth's reputation is strong for supporting good health and preventing connective tissue problems. Who needs chondroitin sulfate supplements when you can make bone broth inexpensively from bones, joints, and meats... and just drink it? "Let food be thy medicine and medicine be thy food." - remember that famous quote from Hippocrates? We'd all do well to be mindful of that statement.

Do I believe the bone broth hype? Yeah, I do. There's no denying that bone broth has nutrients and some of those are a bit unique. Bone broth becomes a way to regularly get those nutrients. So, if your diet is a little unhealthy, or has room for improvement, then bone broth will help. It offers you something nutritious. And, if consumed on a regular basis, I'm hard pressed to not believe those unique ingredients (noted below) won't help. They can! When replacing unhealthy foods with bone broth, you get the best of both worlds. You're reducing inflammatory junk foods in your diet, which facilitates healing. Plus, you're replacing them by consuming something with nutrition. Win-Win.

Bone Broth Basic Nutrition

Depending on the bones used... bone broth typically has nutrients from three main sources:

- Bone
- Marrow
- Connective tissue

Minerals

Bones have a variety of minerals and electrolytes such as calcium, sodium, magnesium, potassium, sulphur and phosphorus that find their way into the broth. These are good for overall health, including, but not limited to, teeth, bones, and heart health. It should be noted that it's the combination of these nutrients contributing to things like building healthy and strong bones, not just because there is some calcium. It's often an erroneous claim that bone broth's bone building comes from calcium; bone broth actually doesn't have that much calcium. Rather, it's the combination of bio-available nutrients and minerals synergistically working their powers on making your skeleton Terminator-level strong.

Arginine

Arginine gives your immune system a nice boost. It also speeds wound healing (that's cool), helps kidney health, helps production of sperm for fertility, and also assists with the production of growth hormone.

Glycine

Glycine is important for many reasons, most notably to help make other amino acids. It also helps your body make heme, it detoxifies, and it enhances digestion. Glycine is also a neurotransmitter that can improve sleep, improve memory, and enhance performance with its calming effects. By getting better sleep, you can better heal your body overall, and lower stress hormones. Lowering stress hormones is vital for optimal health. I will venture to say that this could be one of the keys to bone broth being so healthy for us - giving us nutrients that help us reduce the effects of stress on our bodies.

Glutamine

Glutamine is actually an existing amino acid in our body, and it's a conditionally essential amino acid. This means that an ill or stressed person may not be able to make their own glutamine, or not enough. Glutamine is known for facilitating gut healing, muscle building (athletes love it), and boosting metabolism, all while helping to protect the gut lining, too. Back in my bodybuilding days, we used to supplement with glutamine. It was known to help gain muscle strength, prevent muscle breakdown, and improve endurance. I wish I knew back then what I know now... bone broth supplies it. I could have saved a lot of money by making bone broth and drinking it along with all those whey protein shakes.

Proline

Proline helps heal the digestive tract and improves nutrient absorption. It supports the immune system and metabolism. Proline can also help protect the cardiovascular system by keeping arteries from stiffening. It's associated with beauty, as it might help reduce cellulite and make your skin more supple. Also, proline is known for healing joints and helping cartilage to regenerate. If you've had joint problems, bone broth is an absolute no-brainer.

Bone Broth Body Specifics

When looking at specific areas of the body where bone broth could help, I find the biggest contenders to be: joints, digestion, immune system, and overall inflammation. (Beauty and weight-loss too, but I'll discuss those in the next sections.)

Joints

Bone broth can support joints, muscles, and bone health. When you drink this delicious elixir, you're getting glucosamine and chondroitin, which are touted for helping joints. Glucosamine works by stimulating the growth of new collagen, repairing damaged joints, and reducing pain and inflammation. But to get these results, you can't just drink bone broth now and then – you must make it a regular staple in your diet and daily routine. And, again, when you're consuming bone broth regularly, you're likely eating fewer inflammatory foods at the same time! Therefore, overall, the combo of bone broth and eating better will do wonders for your joints.

Gelatin, which is also found in bone broth, provides building blocks needed to form and maintain strong bones. This helps take pressure off aging joints, and supports healthy bone mineral density. Research shows that the majority of athletes supplementing with collagen saw improvements in joint comfort, and a decrease in factors that negatively impact their performance. There are other ways to get gelatin, but you might as well get it along with your collagen and a host of other beneficial goodies by sipping bone broth regularly.

Digestion Health

Bone broth is easy to digest, so it's perfect for people who are sick, have sensitive stomachs, or conditions like celiac disease. In fact, it's one of the main foods recommended for people who become ill because it's so easy on the stomach while still packing dense nutrition. Bone broth even used to be called "beef tea" and served to invalids for its health and healing elements.

As far back as 1860, Florence Nightingale said, "Beef tea may be chosen as an illustration of great nutrient power in sickness. There is a certain reparative quality in it — we do not know what — as there is in tea; but it may be safely given in almost any inflammatory disease... where much nourishment is required."

According to experts, not only is bone broth easily digested, but it can actually help heal the gut. The gelatin in bone broth soothes gut inflammation. According to Dr. Mercola, "The gelatin found in bone broth is a hydrophilic colloid. It attracts and holds liquids, including digestive juices, thereby supporting proper digestion."

Although not always recognized in conventional medicine circles, the term "leaky gut" is common in alternative groups. It's used to describe a condition where the gut wall is inflamed, and, as a result, it's thought that undigested proteins can pass through, creating inflammation in the body. The thinking goes that, when the gut is healed, then overall inflammation in the body is reduced. Bone broth has a reputation for dramatically helping this. It's believed that the gelatin and collagen in bone broth protects and heals the lining of the digestive tract. Furthermore, as mentioned earlier, the glutamine found in bone broth is thought to be used by the gut to repair the intestinal lining.

Anti-viral

It probably comes as no surprise that bone broth reduces the length of colds and flu. Most of us grew up with our mom serving us chicken soup when we got sick. And... we got better. Now, we know why. Though mom might not have known the mechanism, she was surely raised the same and healed faster from it, too, making it a tradition passed down through the ages.

Chicken soup has such a reputation for being used to heal sickness, that it was once lovingly dubbed "Jewish penicillin." During respiratory infections, it reduces the number of white blood cells, which are the cells that cause flu and cold symptoms. Chicken also contains a natural amino acid called cysteine, which can thin the mucus in your lungs and make it less sticky so you can expel it more easily. It can open up the airways better than hot water.

According to Dr. Axe, "A study of chicken soup (broth) conducted by the University of Nebraska Medical Center wondered what it was in the soup that made it so beneficial for colds and flu. Researchers found that the amino acids that were produced when making chicken stock reduced inflammation in the respiratory system and improved digestion."

Today, in an effort to speed healing, people find themselves reaching for the medicine cabinet when the answer can be found in the kitchen. Move over Tylenol, Tums, and cough syrup. It's time for age-old remedies again.

Chapter 3

BONE BROTH FOR BEAUTY

Anti-aging, anyone? Bone broth is bonafide beauty food. In fact, many women cheer that it's better than Botox! When you look at all of the nutrients that make up bone broth, it would make sense to expect delayed wrinkles, reduction in cellulite, stronger teeth, glowing skin, fast-growing and healthy lush hair, and strong nails.

According to Dr. Kellyann Petrucci,

> "Bone broth is catching on because people know that it tastes fantastic and keeps them healthy. But bone broth isn't just warming and nutritious; it actually turns back the clock. As a weight-loss and anti-aging expert, I've made bone broth a core of my program for years — and it works. I've used it to help dangerously obese patients take off hundreds of pounds, and these days I'm using it to help Hollywood celebrities smooth their wrinkles and sculpt perfect bodies."

But, let's not forget that, although bone broth might support all of these things, its consumption will be largely wasted unless you:

1. Drink enough (usually 1 to 2 cups daily), and
2. Stop eating other offending anti-inflammatory foods.

I'll say it again for emphasis: One reason bone broth is effective when consumed regularly is that you stop reaching for chips and cookies when you have a belly full of delicious warm bone broth. So, both directly and indirectly, expect to feel and look more beautiful when you consistently consume bone broth.

According to Donna Gates, author of Body Ecology, bone broth decreases the appearance of cellulite and makes your skin more supple and smooth-looking. Bone broth contains a compound called hyaluronic acid, which is the primary ingredient in dermal fillers for anti-aging. It's also a key nutrient for helping your skin retain moisture for that dewy, youthful, supple glow we all yearn for.

Plenty of people sing the praises of bone broth helping their beauty. Again, though, you've got to drink enough of it. I suspect that naysayers of bone broth's beauty benefits aren't consuming adequate amounts to actually make a difference. And the bone broth praisers, who are properly enjoying it frequently, are the proof in the pudding that it works.

Dr. Kellyann Petrucci says,

> "While prepping backstage for a recent appearance on The Doctors, a producer asked, 'What in the world do you do to look so young?' I'd already told her my real age, and now she wanted to know why I didn't look my age. The secret? I sip myself young, drinking my way to younger-looking skin and a youthful body. And I use the same 'trick' to trim years off my patients' faces and figures too."

One of bone broth's promised beauty nutrients is collagen. Collagen gives your skin its elasticity. As we lose collagen through natural aging, the skin becomes thinner and creases (ergo, wrinkles form). So, if you want to reduce wrinkles (or prevent them), you have to increase your collagen levels. You can work on this by regularly drinking bone broth, which will give you collagen.

Here's an interesting description of a study done with hairless mice, UV exposure, and gelatin.

According to the Hello Beautiful website:

> "... researchers at Tokyo University of Agriculture and Technology studied the effects of eating gelatin on skin that was repeatedly exposed to ultraviolet light.
>
> "They used three separate groups of hairless mice. The first group was not exposed to the ultraviolet light. The second group was exposed to the light, repeatedly each day with the intensity increased over time.
>
> "The third group received the same amount of exposure to the ultraviolet light as the second group. However, the third group was also given a portion of gelatin to eat each day.
>
> "What they found was that the mice exposed to the light without the gelatin had a 53% average decrease in the collagen content of their skin, compared to the mice that received no ultraviolet light exposure at all. Astonishingly, the mice that were exposed to the light, but also fed gelatin had no collagen decrease at all. They actually had an average collagen increase of 17%."

Now, I know the mice weren't sipping bone broth while lounging around in velour robes... they're hairless and probably cold after all. Instead, they were given collagen supplements. Further, they're mice and not human. But the results are still interesting and make me run for the bone broth (or maybe that's just confirmation bias). Heck, I wonder how the results might have been different if the mice *were* sipping bone broth with all of the extra nutrients that come with it instead of just an isolated supplement of collagen (that's a funny thing to picture ... little mice sitting around sipping bone broth from tiny, little mice-sized mugs).

It's true that some foods contain nutrients, such as vitamin C, that *help stimulate* collagen production, don't actually contain collagen themselves. Drinking bone broth takes care of that, because you're actually drinking collagen. Further, if you do want extra collagen in your diet, in addition to bone broth, you can supplement with the form of collagen hydrolysate (hydrolyzed collagen) or collagen peptides. In fact, you can add quick-dissolving collagen powder to your mug of bone broth and reap a big collagen boost. That's bone broth on steroids. You can also use these convenient, commercial collagen products in coffee, tea, or just drinking them in water to get added collagen to your diet (they're colorless, tasteless, and odorless). These are available in the protein powder section of many health food stores as well as Amazon.com.

More on collagen benefits, this time with humans...

Dr. J. Axe shares on his website,

> "Double-blind, placebo-controlled studies investigating the age-defending properties of collagen have found that 2.5 to 5 grams of collagen hydrolysate (CH), used among women aged 35–55 once daily for eight weeks, supports skin elasticity, skin moisture, trans-epidermal water loss (dryness) and skin roughness. At the end of only four weeks, those using collagen showed a statistically significant improvement in comparison to those using a placebo, with regard to skin moisture and skin evaporation, plus noticeable decreases in signs of accelerated aging, all with little to no side effects."

Bone broth for the beauty win. I mean, even at the most simple level, I find the act of sipping delicious and comforting bone broth to be good for my soul as it reduces stress. This alone is good for our beauty and preventing furrow lines.

Chapter 4

BONE BROTH FOR WEIGHT LOSS

Losing Weight with Bone Broth

Many people use bone broth to help them lose weight. Some dramatically so. If you need to lose a few pounds, then simply replacing unhealthy snacks with bone broth can do the trick. If you have more than a few pounds to lose, then consider a bone broth fast. We'll cover both of these approaches in detail.

Bone Broth for Snack Time!

Instead of snacking on unhealthy things like chips or cookies, treat yourself to a mug of salty bone broth. It's satisfying on many levels, and equally important, it's effective. The simple tactic is it can help you feel full, so you're not reaching for carb-crappy snacks. This alone may be one of the reasons so many people report losing weight drinking bone broth. At the most basic level, you're simply consuming nourishing and satiating soup, thereby helping you reduce nutrient-deplete-shit-snack-foods in your everyday diet.

The plan for weight loss: Make a mug of bone broth for your daily

11am and 3 pm snacks. That's it. If you're not a snacker and you still need to lose weight, I'll venture to say that your meals aren't as healthy as they should be, or the portions are too large. In either case, adding bone broth as an appetizer to your meals will help you eat less of the food that you shouldn't be eating.

However, if your usual itch is to grab unhealthy foods later in the day, say, a couple of hours after dinner while you're watching TV, then have a mug of bone broth at that time instead. Even if you want something sweet or different than bone broth, make a deal with yourself that you'll first have a mug of bone broth. If, after that, you still want something else, then you can consider it. However, I can tell you from experience, that once you've had a delicious mug of bone broth, you probably won't crave anything else. Or, if you are, the craving will be greatly reduced.

Bone Broth Fast

Need to lose more than a little weight? Some people take things to the next level with bone broth by doing a "bone broth fast," meaning you consume nothing but bone broth for some period of time. Some people do a shorter fast to simply drop a few pounds quickly. Maybe you have an event or trip that you want to drop a few pounds for... a quick bone broth fast (1 to 2 days) can help you reach that weight loss goal. Other people go longer, for more ambitious weigh loss goals. Either way, bone broth fasting can be a meaningful way to keep your weight under control.

For most people, the mere thought of fasting makes them want to run. But fasting with bone broth is completely different. Broth is tasty and you'll actually find it a treat to consume it all day. Still... fasting, I know... it's not fun. However, it can have many health benefits, only one of which is speedy weight loss. So you might want to be a badass and consider it. If you're a foodie who can't imagine parting with food for more than 8 hours, but you want to lose weight, a bone broth fast (with a day of Netflix binge-watching) could be just the ticket. It's all about setting yourself up for success (that's the Netflix part).

The main reasons people endure fasting is to:

- Lose weight
- Increase focus
- Reduce fasting insulin levels
- Promote the secretion of human growth hormone (helpful for burning fat)
- Normalizing appetite through hunger hormones, such as ghrelin
- Longevity

Those are all really good reasons to do a fast. Fasting can be a real boon to your health. The good news is that a bone broth fast makes fasting more tolerable. Fasting isn't easy for people, myself included (um... hello... hunger?). However, bone broth is satisfying (and nourishing) so it makes it easier to get through a day of not eating when you get to enjoy delicious bone broth. One of the things that makes a bone broth fast stand apart from other types of fasts is that it's a good way to obtain more collagen, a type of protein needed to create healthy tissue found throughout the body. Reducing excessive body-fat and wrinkles at the same time? Score!

If you're interested in doing a bone broth fast, you can start by doing it just one day a week. Or, if you're after more dramatic results, start with two to three days per week. Either way, make sure your doctor gives you the go-ahead for fasting, because fasting isn't appropriate for everyone.

Bone Broth Fasting Plan

Each day of the bone broth fast, you should consume 3 to 4 quarts of bone broth. You can have a slow cooker going all day for this, but I find that a bone broth fast is easiest if I already have everything made and ready to warm up and drink. I'll be damned if I'm going to be in the middle of fast, feel hungry, and then have to wait, like, 8 hours to make broth! No thank you. Be prepared.

Therefore, when I plan a 1-day bone broth fast, I take a day (prior to the start of the fast) to make a big batch, at least 4 quarts. I divide the bone broth into 8 pint-sized, glass mason jars. I store them in the refrigerator. If you want to do a multi-day fast, then prepare the appropriate amount of bone broth for each day of the fast (in advance if desired).

When you make bone broth, fat rises to the top and it can be easily separated once it's cool. When fasting, I personally prefer to leave some of the fat in the broth. When the fat rises to the top while it's cooling, I keep most of it there (it goes back into the broth when heated).

If you choose to remove all of the fat, however, it would be a much more calorie-restricted fast. This will speed weight loss, but you'll also be more hungry. Experiment and see what works best for you. I leave the fat in because the fat is healthy and it also keeps me satisfied longer so the fast isn't as difficult. One way to approach a multi-day bone broth fast is to keep the fat in your bone broth for the first day or two, as you adjust to being on a liquid fast. Then, start reducing the fat or cut it out completely for the last day(s) of the fast.

When it comes time to warm the broth during the fast, I simply empty the contents of a one-pint jar (broth and fat) into a small soup pot or sauce pan. I heat it up, add a pinch of sea salt, and enjoy. I like storing the broth in the pint-sized jars, because I only want to drink two cups at a time. That's what fits in my favorite mug. A good rule of thumb is to drink a pint every 2 to 3 hours, or as desired.

Some people like doing a 24-hour fast once or twice a week for weight loss. Then, after desired weight loss is achieved you can decrease to a 24-hour bone broth fast once every couple weeks or once a month.

Finally, if you want to do a fast, but don't want to be troubled with making the broth, Dr. KellyAnn has a selection of bone broth products for sale on her website, DrKellyAnnStore.com. One in particular is called "SLIM Collagen Broth to Go." I've never tried it, but it gets good reviews.

PART II

HOW TO MAKE & USE BONE BROTH

Chapter 5

USING BONE BROTH

Convenience

Convenience is one of the top reasons to use bone broth. True, you have to make it first, but it's very easy to make, as you'll see in the rest of the book. Whether you buy pre-made bone broth or make it yourself, having it available to drink as a quick snack, or part of a meal, is where the convenience really comes in. It's especially helpful when you live a busy life.

- You can take bone broth on the road, just like you would with coffee or tea in a travel mug. Keep this in mind for your morning commute. Or even your next road trip.
- You can also take bone broth to work in a big-ass thermos. It will stay warm and you can sip it all day long. There's no need to waste time making a lunch for work. You can easily warm up some broth, and take it to go.
- When you make bone broth regularly, you'll always have a supply in the refrigerator, or at the very least in the freezer. It becomes an easy food to have for quick soups and stews, or

simply drinking it by the mug. Regular bone broth drinkers such as myself find themselves craving it if they go too many days without it.

- Camping! If you're a camper, then you have to take bone broth with you next time. If you keep batches of it frozen, you can put these in the cooler in place of some of the ice. The use of it is two-fold... keep things cool in the cooler and provide food. That said, if you're a camper with limited cooler space, consider making homemade dehydrated bone broth powder (see recipes, chapter 8). You can also buy it in convenient little packages at: https://www.drkellyannstore.com/products/slim-collagen-broth-to-go

- It's as convenient as a Starbucks Via coffee, and much better for you.

How to Use Bone Broth

There are so many ways to use bone broth, you'll wonder how you ever got along without it.

Drinking Bone Broth Solo

In our family, we drink bone broth regularly, by its delicious self, in a mug. I heat it on my stove and stir in sea salt. Sometimes I use plain sea salt and other times I add smoked sea salt when I'm feeling fancy. You can get creative with different salt flavors and salts from around the world. Sometimes, I stir in freshly chopped herbs. It's delicious. Bone broth is very inexpensive to make, and can be a healthy addition to your family's diet. The common "prescription" is to drink 1 to 2 mugs a day (sometimes more) for the best health benefiting results.

Use Bone Broth for Other Recipes

You may have been initially drawn to bone broth for its health benefits, but WOWZA, using it in other recipes might just become your favorite reason to have bone broth on hand in your kitchen at all times. It makes everything so good! Get used to regular compliments on your food when you do this. Even better? Using bone broth in cooking other foods is another way to get more of bone broth's healing and anti-aging benefits in your body. So, drinking bone broth by the mug gets it into your body, and when you also use it to cook, you're getting even more of it in your body that way, too. Super flavored foods plus super nutrition.

Soups, Stews, Grains, Etc.

The primary means by which I use bone broth for cooking is to replace boring ol' water in recipes that call for water. This trick works fantastically well in soups, stews, chilis, gravies, sauces, mashed veggies, rice, pasta, grains, etc. Moreover, it bears repeating that this is the best way to take your meals to a new level of depth and flavor. For this reason, I always have bone broth either cooking in some appliance on my kitchen counter, fresh in the refrigerator, or in the freezer, ready to thaw and use.

Demi-Glace

Another way to use bone broth is to reduce it down to a demi-glace or use it to make a pan-sauce. Demi-glace is a beautifully rich, glossy brown sauce in French cuisine that is made from bone broth. It's the backbone of the world's most famous sauces. You simply simmer bone broth down, and, as the water evaporates, the flavors are concentrated and intensified. (Keep an eye on it though so it doesn't burn.) Drizzle your demi-glace over your next steak or chicken roast, and be prepared for your eyes to roll back in your head. Better yet, serve it to guests... they will be blown away. Seriously.

Pan Sauce

You can use bone broth to make a pan sauce. First, you'll cook a piece of meat (steak or chicken, for example). Here's how:

- Get your pan hot, add a drizzle of olive oil or a teaspoonful of ghee.
- Put the meat in, let it get a good sear and flip it (1 to 2 minutes for beef, 3 to 6 minutes for chicken). It should release easily from the pan. If it sticks, let it cook a bit longer.
- Flip and let the other side get a good sear (same times).
- Lower the heat and cook until the meat reaches your desired temperature.
- Remove the meat and set aside.

Now your pan will have delicious little bits of cooked meat and flavor inside it, but it's stuck to the pan. Turn the heat back up and add a 1/4 cup of bone broth to the pan. Deglaze the pan by using a spatula to scrape up the bits as the broth loosens them. Simmer to let it reduce and thicken a bit, season with salt and pepper, and pour over the meat you set aside. (Tip: You can make it a buttery sauce by adding a pat of butter, a minute or so after you add the broth to the pan, using a whisk to mix them while they collectively help you remove the flavor bits from the skillet.)

Frozen Bone Brothsicles

When I first started consuming bone broth many years ago, my daughter was only 3 years old at the time. I wanted her to experience the benefits of it, but she was too young to sit down to a hot mug of bone broth, because, well, it's hot. For her, we actually did the opposite. I froze the bone broth in fun silicone molds of different shapes. We would take a few out of the freezer, cut them into bone broth ice chunks and put them in a bowl with a spoon. She still loves her bone brothsicle. You could also use a Popsicle mold and freeze bone broth in them for frozen bone broth on a stick.

Bone Broth as a Coffee Alternative

Some people claim beef bone broth is becoming the new coffee. I have my doubts because it's just not coffee(!), but I'm open-minded. The people making these claims say the bone broth's nutrients perk you up. Hmmm... maybe. If it's replacing a donut, then sure. Replacing coffee? I'm not quite convinced it's going to give the same buzz as a caffeine-rich cup of java.

My recommendation: If you like a caffeine boost in the morning, then enjoy your coffee and have a cup of bone broth after, instead of that second cup of coffee. Or, have coffee with commercially prepared collagen protein powder stirred in. It won't have all the same nutrition as bone broth, but it does amp your coffee with some skin-beautifying and joint-strengthening protein.

See the Chapter 8 for groovy bone broth beverage ideas!

Pregnant or Nursing?

Bone broth is, however, a great alternative to coffee for pregnant and nursing women. It doesn't have caffeine, but it's a deliciously warm drink that nourishes you and, indirectly, your baby. This can make the fact that you can't drink caffeine... easier to swallow, as it were.

Furthermore, there is the bonus of the potential skin-tightening ingredients in bone broth to keep a mama's skin healthy, during and after pregnancy. Because collagen helps maintain the skin's smoothness and elasticity, it makes sense that it could be used for combating stretch marks that can result from pregnancy.

Lastly, and importantly, drinking bone broth during pregnancy also helps nourish the growing baby. Not only that, but women experiencing nausea with pregnancy often have a hard time keeping food down. Bone broth can help this. It's gentle on the stomach and nutritious at the same time.

Chapter 6

MAKING BONE BROTH

The Bone Broth Basics

Now that we've established drinking bone broth could be a great boon to your health, let's talk about how you make it.

Making bone broth is as simple as putting bones (knuckles and joints, too, if you have them) along with optional muscle meats, cartilage, tendons/ligaments, skin, organ meats, vegetables, and/or spices, and water into a cooking appliance like a slow cooker, Sous Vide Supreme, pressure cooker, or a good ol' stock pot. If you don't have any of these items, but you have a regular soup pot, that will work, too.

The variation of ingredients for your broth is up to you. Your bone broth can be super simple or creatively complex. When I first started making bone broth, I enjoyed making different broths, enhanced by a myriad of flavors. I've used ginger and cinnamon sticks. I've use different mushrooms. I dug into my pantry for longevity tonic herbs, too. Sometimes, I even added tea bags toward the end of cooking for a few minutes. Just look in your spice cabinet and let your imagination run wild.

Your main bone broth options are:

- Chicken bone broth
- Beef bone broth
- Pork bone broth
- Fish bone broth

But you can also use lamb bones (and meats), veal, rabbit, quail, duck, turkey, and venison. Some people make a vegan option which is using only vegetables, but that doesn't have the nourishment from the bones, nor the intensely rewarding flavor.

Below, you'll read some quick pointers that will help, depending on the particular kind of bones you're using.

Chicken (or Turkey or Duck) Bone Broth

I love making chicken bone broth because its taste is my favorite when drinking it by the mug. It's also my favorite for cooking rice. I think most people are familiar with chicken bone broth, because it's given to people in times of cold-n-flu sickness for its healing benefits. Who doesn't remember childhood days of staying home from school with a cold, watching TV, and eating chicken noodle soup?

With chicken bone broth, you'll typically use the bones of chicken that you've already cooked. For example, if you roasted (or baked) a chicken, you'll use the leftover bones. However, you can also use uncooked, raw bones, including chicken feet (and backs) to make the broth. Chicken feet are one of the most special parts of chicken bone broth because they contribute loads of collagen. I remember when I used to work in Hong Kong, it was common at dim sum to see chicken feet on people's plates. They would gnaw and suck on them like there was gold to be had. At the time, sadly, twenty-something me was totally grossed out by it. Today, I'd be the first in line!

Unfortunately, chicken feet aren't easy to come by in the United

States. When I've included them in my chicken bone broth, I ordered them online, delivered frozen. They only required a quick rinse before using them. Because chicken feet are hard to get, I don't include them as often as I'd like.

Chicken bones are small so you'll need a lot if you want to make a big batch of bone broth. The best plan is to keep a stash of bones in your freezer every time you roast a chicken. Once you have a few carcasses stored up, then you can commence with making your bone broth. Conversely, you can make a small batch of bone broth from just one chicken carcass. It's common for me to go around and collect bones from my family after a chicken dinner, and toss them into a stove pot or my Instant Pot. I'll make a quart (or two) in a jiffy, giving me nourishing broth to enjoy the next day.

Or, here's another thing I do for quick chicken broth: I love roasting a couple of packages of drumsticks (or chicken thighs) at a time, which my family of three will polish off for lunch. I take the bones and put them in a little soup pot, add water, and simply let them cook for 3 to 4 hours. You'll note that isn't very long and the length of time I do this depends on how much time I have. The point is that you can be flexible. While most people cook the bones for up to 24 hours, sometimes I just do it for a few hours. I can then use the broth in that night's dinner or put it in the refrigerator to enjoy the next day.

Keeping it simple like this, I can also make bone broth when I travel, if there's a kitchen. When I only have a few hours and small stash of bones, I can freeze them for later cooking or I can make a quick quart of broth right then. Just because I don't have my pressure cooker or a proper stock pot with me doesn't stop me. You can definitely make broth when you're traveling so long as you have a small pot, some chicken bones, and a refrigerator (unless you plan to drink it straight from the pot - I've done that!). Oh, and a stove.

Typically, however, when making chicken bone broth, you cook it for 12 to 24 hours in a slow cooker, stock pot, Sous Vide Supreme (water oven), or a pressure cooker (the time is MUCH shorter in a pressure cooker - approximately 60 minutes).

Making chicken bone broth takes less time than making beef bone broth, so that's one of the advantages of using chicken.

Beef (or Veal or Lamb) Bone Broth

My preference for beef (or veal or lamb) broth comes when I'm using it for cooking recipes like stews, gravies, sauces, etc. Beef bone broth is also great to make soup and rice with it.

Beef bones can be purchased directly from your butcher or grocery store's meat department. If you don't see them, just ask!

Beef bone broth, like chicken, can be made with both raw or roasted bones. My strong preference, however, with beef bone broth, is to roast the bones first. I don't care for the taste of beef bone broth made with raw bones.

For beef bones, they're much bigger than chicken bones, and especially so if using knuckles and joints (which I recommend using, when possible, for ultimate nutrition). Because of their size, you'll want to use a large enough cooking vessel, such as a large stock pot, 8-quart slow cooker, or Sous Vide Supreme.

Beef bone broth is best when you cook it for 24 to 48 hours. The flavor is the best, not only when using roasted bones, but also if you include bones with some meat on them. On occasion, for added flavor, I've even added cooked ground beef (or stew beef), which I later strained out.

Pork Bone Broth

Making bone broth with pork bones isn't super common, but it should be. It's delicious, nutritious, and easy all the same. In fact, as more people are making bone broth, beef bones are going up a bit in price. The days of getting beef bones from the butcher for cheap are nearly gone. However, pork bones are still pretty cheap, because not as many people think to use them for bone broth. So, again, if you don't see them, just ask!

Some people favor pork bone broth for the flavor and find that, once they start making it, it's all they want to make. My amazing local butcher sells pork bone broth that she makes herself (yes, a she-butcher, which is as cool as it is rare). If we don't make our own, we love buying hers. I'll use pork bone broth when cooking a beef chuck roast. OMG-A-mazing combination of sultry, rich flavors.

The same rules for cooking times and roasting bones for beef apply to pork bones. Roast those bones and cook them in water for 24 to 48 hours.

Fish Bone Broth

Fish broth is delicate. When comparing traditional cooking times between fish, chicken, and beef (when using a stove), fish is the fastest – less than one hour. The stove is also the recommended way to cook fish bone broth because it takes so little time.

When making fish bone broth, be sure to include the whole fish head and all the bones. It's also important to use only non-oily fish, to prevent the oils from getting rancid while cooking. Consider rockfish, halibut, turbot, tilapia, wild Pacific cod, or sole. Since you don't typically see fish bones or carcasses in display cases of the fish department, simply ask the fishmonger to save the heads and carcasses for you. They're usually happy to oblige.

With fish bone broth, the bones are delicate and small, and you don't want to overcook them. Use a soup (or stock) pot on the stove. You don't need to roast the bones, and you can simmer it for as little as 20 minutes before it's ready to be strained (fish carcasses and fish head discarded). Don't cook more than 60 minutes.

You can then use the broth. Fish bone broth is a great way to quickly add flavor to a soup or meal. It's also wonderful for making coconut or Thai-inspired dishes. You might add some seaweed, such as a couple of pieces of dulse or kombu. This will increase the iodine in the broth even more, which is an important nutrient for health and energy.

Mixed Meat Bone Broth

There's nothing wrong with mixing bones of different animals (except fish). If you have a freezer full of chicken, pork, and beef bones, feel free to add them all to the same pot. (Cook the bone broth for about 24 hours – roughly the max time for chicken and the least time for the beef and pork.)

Liver and Other Organ Meats?

In theory, there's nothing wrong with adding liver and other organ meats to your bone broth. That said, I've never done it, because I already eat enough organ meats separately (strictly for nutrition), I don't like the taste, and it would seem like a criminal act to make something so yummy and delicious as bone broth taste even a little bit like liver. Yuck. But to each his/her own. If you love the flavor, go ahead and give it a try!

Vegetable Non-Bone Broth

Though I'm not an advocate of plain vegetable broth, because it's usually weak in flavor and doesn't offer much in the way of nutrition, many people add vegetables to their bone broth. This is totally optional. It's common practice to use whatever left-over veggies you find in the refrigerator that are on their last day or beyond their prime. Some vegetables can enhance the color of the broth, depending on which ones you use. For example, beets and red onions will impart a slightly red color to the broth.

The best vegetables are the ones that can stand up to the long cooking. This means hearty veggies like root vegetables, onions, etc. Avoid using green vegetables, as they can't withstand the extended cooking process. They become too mushy and bitter. Herbs are good additions to broth, but only add them during the last hour of cooking, to prevent bitterness.

My common M.O. these days is actually just making bone broth with nothing but water and bones. Simple. I don't want to be troubled with timing the addition of herbs or adding vegetables. I also prefer the meatiest, deepest-flavored broth I can make. Moreover, adding nothing but bones keeps things extra easy because you don't need to strain extra gunk out at harvest time. The less there is to strain out, the easier it is. The easier it is, the more often you'll make it, and the bigger the benefits you'll experience.

If you want more diversity to your bone broth, but still want to keep it fairly easy to strain, then add things like garlic cloves, a quartered onion or two (skin and all), and bay leaves. (More about this, below.)

Vinegar and Wine

Adding 1 to 2 tablespoons of vinegar is popular to help better extract the minerals out of the bones and into your broth. You can use apple cider vinegar, balsamic vinegar, wine vinegar, or rice vinegar. I did that all the time when I was first learning to make bone broth years ago, but it does sometimes alter the flavor too much for my liking. Therefore, if I use a medium like that, I reach for wine. Wine is purported to do the same thing (extract minerals), but adds a nicer flavor. But neither are really necessary, in my opinion. I don't imagine our great ancestors used apple cider vinegar when they made their healing pots of bone broth.

That said, if I use wine, I don't use "cooking" wine. When I cook with wine, I use a good quality wine that I like to drink. And, wine in bone broth is fabulous for flavor. I generally use the following pairings (or whatever I have on hand):

- Chicken bone broth: white wine
- Beef bone broth: red wine
- Pork bone broth: rosé wine
- Fish bone broth: white wine

These are suggestions only. Any which way you use wine, it'll taste great.

Cold Water Start

Many people, especially chefs trained in French classic cooking, will start the bone broth with cold water. The cold start and slow heating separates soluble from solid proteins. Basically, this allows any impurities in the bones to rise to the surface, where they can be easily skimmed off with a spoon. I'll be honest, I don't make sure to start with cold all the time; I just use whatever temperature is flowing from my tap, which is usually coolish to room temperature. During summer in Arizona, my tap water never comes out cooler than warm.

No Salt!

Thou shalt not salt the broth in the cooking phase! (You salt bone broth when you drink with it or cook with it.)

I repeat... Don't salt the bone broth while cooking, because you'll often want to use the bone broth in another recipe. If it's salted, it can ruin the other recipe. Or, if you let it reduce too much while cooking, it concentrates the salt and you might have to throw out the whole batch. Make your bone broth unsalted, and then simply salt it before drinking or using, as needed. I repeat, *don't use salt in the cooking process!*

Note: If you taste your broth during or after cooking, don't expect a full, delicious flavor. It will taste quite bland. The flavor explodes later on, when you add the salt.

Include These for Extra gelatin, Marrow, and Flavor

When possible, I recommend adding bones and parts that include beef knuckles and joints (for beef bone broth) and chicken/pork feet (for chicken or pork bone broth). This ensures your bone broth contains extra gelatin. All of these valuable parts contain high amounts of collagen and cartilage. Moreover, shank and leg bones offer plenty of bone marrow, which also provides health benefits. The consensus is that bones and knuckles give the bone broth "body" while the meat (like soup meat or oxtails) gives "flavor." In a perfect bone-broth-world, you'd use a mixture of bones. In the real world, my broths are generally made from just plain marrow bones. On those occasions when I'm lucky enough to find knuckles or feet, I use them, but they're not always available so no biggie. My bone broth will have plenty of anti-aging and health-boosting properties. And you can always compensate by simply making and drinking more of the stuff.

Remove the Scum

As the bone broth is cooking, if you notice a scum of dirty-looking bubbles rising to the top of the cooking vessel, simply skim it off with a spoon and discard it. Not all bone broth produces this. The scum is not to be confused with the "skin" though. Once broth is cooked (or cooking) you might see a skin forming on the top and some consider this the best part. According to Dr. Mercola, "It contains valuable nutrients, such as sulfur, along with healthful fats, so just stir it back into the broth."

Eating Any Remaining Meat

If you have bones that have some meat on them – such as chicken, or oxtail – then once the broth is done cooking (or even during the cooking), you can enjoy the leftover meat. Ideally, you should remove the meat after it had been cooking an hour or two (maybe more for beef, depending on the cut), and returning the bones to the pot.

By this time, the meat will have imparted its delicious flavor, and you can remove it so it doesn't get too gnarly and tough. This way, you can still enjoy the meat and make use of it as a wonderful and protein-rich food. To do this, you can carefully remove the bones with the meat attached from the cooking broth. Set the meaty bones in a bowl. Once they're cool enough to handle, pull off the meat and set the meat aside. Return the bones to the pot to finish cooking the bone broth.

This can be done when using a stock pot on the stove, a dutch oven in the oven, a slow cooker, or a Sous Vide Supreme. I wouldn't recommend this process when using a pressure cooker, though, because the cooking time is so short on a pressure cooker anyway. Also, you don't want to let all the pressure out midway through the cooking.

The removed meat won't have all its original flavor – because part of the flavor will be in the stock – but it's still pretty yummy!

You can enjoy the meat in a few ways. You can eat it right then, all by itself (that's my habit). Or you could add it on top of some scrambled eggs or cooked buttery rice. Finally, you can consider adding it back to the broth to make a meatier soup, once the broth is done cooking. To do this, simply refrigerate the meat while you wait for the bone broth to finish cooking. Once it's done, stir the meat back in and enjoy.

Storing Bone Broth

You have three options for storing bone broth:

- Refrigerator
- Freezer
- Pantry

In the refrigerator, it'll stay fresh for up to 5 days. If you freeze it, you can usually count on it staying flavorful for up to 6 months. In the pantry, you can store dehydrated bone broth for years, if properly stored. See recipe for Dehydrated Broth Powder in Chapter 8.

Bone Broth Flavor Options

Here is a list of things I've added to bone broth on different occasions for variety and fun. These things can be added at the beginning of cooking, during the second half of cooking, or in some cases, during the last hour of cooking. As mentioned above, some people add veggies during the last hours of cooking, as that's all it takes to extract most of the flavor and any potential nutrients.

Keep in mind, you can always add things to the bone broth when you serve it. For example, you might leave out the vegetables while the bone broth is cooking, but when you warm it up to serve, you could add spiralized carrots and thinly sliced celery, cooking them in the bone broth right before serving.

Cinnamon Sticks - Toss 1 to 3 cinnamon sticks in with the bones, depending on the quantity you're making. And, well, how much you like cinnamon. This is especially nice in beef bone broth.

Ginger Root and Turmeric Root - When you're looking for a spicy, extra warming soup, ginger is a great addition. As ginger is known for helping with digestion, it just makes sense to add to broth, if that's one of the reasons you're consuming broth. What you might not know is that ginger has been shown to be very helpful for the lungs when they're under attack from cold-n-flu viruses. Next time you're making chicken bone broth (and you're sick with the flu or a cold), be sure to add some ginger to it. And, if you already have your broth made without ginger, then just grate some fresh ginger into it before drinking. Turmeric root, also known for having anti-inflammatory health benefits, can be a smart addition, especially as its deep orange color enhances the color of the broth. You can wash and add the roots whole, just like you bought them. Although, I usually chop them into 1-inch pieces first. These can stay in the whole time the broth is cooking or taken out after a few hours.

Garlic – Adding garlic to bone broth enhances flavor, adds nutrients, and is super easy... literally one of the easiest times you've ever used garlic. Just toss in the whole head, no peeling. Or if you're feeling peppy, slice the head in half, and then toss it in. If you don't want a strong garlic flavor, then you can toss in a couple of cloves instead of a whole head. Again, no peeling or processing required. Pretty neat, huh?

Onions and Shallots - I do love the flavor of onion, so if I add vegetables to my broth, it tends to be onions, shallots, or leeks. Adding onions to broth, like garlic, is easy. Quarter or halve them, and add the whole thing including the skins, to the water and bones. Yes, including the skin. In fact, with red onions, the skins enhance the color of the broth a bit.

Leeks - Another great way to use leeks is adding them to broth. For leeks, you use the whole thing, including the green parts.

Vegetables – As mentioned previously, when adding vegetables to bone broth, it's best to go with hardy varieties like root vegetables. They are tough and can tolerate longer cooking times without turning to goo. Because their job is done within a couple of hours, it's ideal to put them in near the end and then take them out with the bones. However, you can add them in the beginning and try to take them out a couple of hours later. That said, I've been known to just leave them in the whole time. Consider vegetables like: beet, carrot, sweet potato, celery, parsnip, turnip, tomato, celery root, etc.

Sea Veggies (a.k.a. seaweed) - It's nice to add kombu and dulse to any bone broth, not just fish bone broth. Sea vegetables add a bit of salt, but not much, and they don't make it fishy tasting. They lend a nice soft flavor along with iodine. Like regular land vegetables, sea veggies can be added at any time. You can remove them within a couple of hours or keep them in until the end.

Chinese Tonic Medicinal Herbs and Tinctures - You can also use tonic herbs, Chinese medicinal herbs, and even tinctures in your bone broth. The reasons for these are varied. If you're interested in a broth specifically for longevity, like my Longevity Broth (see the recipes in Chapter 8), then consider adding things like ginseng root, Astragalus root, Schisandra berries, chaga mushroom, etc.

You could also look to other unique herbs such as Hawthorn berries, Echinacea root, or even elderberries in whole/dried form, or squirt tinctures into the broth while it's cooking. These are great ways to amp up the healing of bone broth for acute illnesses and for long-term longevity.

Alternatively, if you prefer more flexibility with your bone broth, you can make it plain and squirt tinctures into it just before serving. For example, make the bone broth with just bones and water, and just before serving it, squirt in some Echinacea tincture for cold and flu viruses. You can find just about any kind of tincture in health food stores today. Perhaps a squirt of valerian into your bone broth before bed will help you sleep better. Or a squirt of nettles tincture in your bone broth at lunch.

Dried Hot Chili Peppers - When you want extra spice, add dried hot chili peppers. These can be great to boost the immune system and stimulate your metabolism. This could be especially helpful when doing a bone broth fast for weight loss.

Tea Bags - This is a fun way to change up your bone broth routine, and potentially add a little caffeine if you like drinking your bone broth in the morning. Depending on the size of the batch, I vary the amount from 1 to 4 bags. Kukicha is great, and I've also used chai spiced tea bags. I put the bags into the cooking broth for about 30 to 60 minutes and then pull them out. I drape the strings over the edge of the slow cooker (or stock pot) to make removing them easier. Keep the caffeine content in mind when serving broth that includes tea that might have caffeine. You also have plenty of fun, non-caffeine herbal tea options, such as lemongrass, rooibos, hibiscus, or chamomile.

Coffee - Believe it or not, you can even add some instant coffee like Starbucks Via (or any other brand) to your bone broth. The idea is to enhance it with a hint of coffee, not to make coffee, so go easy on the amount and experiment to get the balance just right. This would go well with beef bone broth.

Lemongrass - When looking for some fabulous Thai-inspired recipes, consider making fish bone broth and adding fresh lemongrass stalks while it simmers. Or try making chicken bone broth and adding lemon grass stalks plus jasmine green tea bags! (To prevent bitterness, only steep green tea bags for a few minutes.)

Whole Cloves - These add a nice spice flavor. Cloves are a wonderful addition to bone broth during the holidays. Roasts made with clove-infused bone broth are perfect for the season!

Wine – As mentioned before, wine can be used in place of vinegar to help extract nutrients from the bones, but of course, it also adds a rich, luxurious flavor. Traditional pairing suggests red wine for beef, lamb, and pork bone broths (or rosé for pork, like I do), and white wine for chicken, duck, turkey, and fish bone broths. It's all good though... it's wine!

Fresh Herbs - Herbs can add lovely flavor to broths. My favorites are thyme and rosemary. They're the hardier of the herbs and can handle being in the broth, releasing their aromatic compounds for an hour or so. Therefore, these are best when added during the last hour of cooking to prevent the bone broth from tasting bitter. For more delicate herbs like fresh basil, cilantro, oregano, and sage, I recommend adding them right before serving. You can do this by chopping the fresh herbs and adding them to the bowl before you enjoy the bone broth. You can also add dried herbs right before serving the bone broth, too. Sometimes, it's perfect to simply stir in some garlic and onion powder for variety.

Tomato Paste - This is terrific when you spread it on the bones *before* you roast them, and I highly recommend trying this at least once. Another option is adding some tomato paste straight to the cooking vessel, while the bone broth is cooking. Tomato paste is usually used for beef or lamb bone broths.

Brown the Bones First by Roasting Them

Brown your bones by roasting them before making broth from them. Also brown your meat, if you'll be including any. This provides the best flavor and a rich, brown color. This applies only to beef, lamb, and pork. Roasting is optional for chicken – not necessary, but not bad either, such as when making broth from the bones of your chicken dinner. Don't roast fish bones prior to making broth from them.

Some people use raw beef bones, but not me. I'll never forget the time when I didn't brown the bones first. I had been cooking the bone broth all night and I opened the bedroom door in the morning and almost gagged at the smell. Shocked and dismayed, I went to the kitchen, opening all windows along the way, while holding my breath, and I unplugged the slow cooker. I had no idea slow cooking raw bones could smell so gross. What would such a horrid-smelling thing taste like? I'll never know; I pitched the whole stinky batch. Never again.

Make sure not to roast more bones than will fit in the cooking appliance you'll be using to make the broth. Those beef knuckles can be really big! If you accidentally roast too many bones, just freeze them and they'll be ready to use the next time you make bone broth. You can put frozen, roasted bones right into the cooking appliance, without thawing them, when you make a batch of bone broth.

I roast my beef bones at 350 to 400 degrees F in an oven for 45 to 60 minutes. It's a good idea to turn the bones (and any meat) over once during roasting. If you're roasting meat along with the bones, and the meat is finished roasting before the bones, remove it and set it aside. Continue roasting the bones until you see a nice caramelized color.

You can even go hotter in temperature for roasting the bones. According to Bon Appétit: "Don't be afraid to really take the bones to the limit: Crank the oven up high – a bold 450°, says senior food editor Andy Baraghani. Lily Freedman, test kitchen contributor, also adds that you have to put in ample oven time. "A quick 15 minutes won't do. Take the bones right up to the edge of '*too done*.'"

Cooking Your Bone Broth

Once the bones are well-browned, use tongs to place them in the bone broth cooking appliance of choice. Pour the fat out of the roasting pan (you can discard this or add it with the bones).

Once the fat is removed, add some water to the roasting pan. Heat the roasting pan over high heat on the stove, and bring the water you added (to the roasting pan) to a simmer. Stir it with a large cooking spoon or spatula to loosen up the coagulated juices and flavor bits. Finally, add this liquid to the pot with the bones.

At this point, you'll add the rest of the water you need to fill the pot with the bones, plus any desired vegetables, etc., and start the bone broth cooking. For further directions, see the sections below for your appliance of choice: slow cooker, Sous Vide Supreme, pressure cooker, stove, or oven.

Harvesting Your Bone Broth – Overview

It doesn't matter which appliance you use for cooking your delicious bone broth – you'll harvest it the same. You essentially just strain everything out (bones, herbs, vegetables) to get your bone broth to a simple, clear liquid.

At it's simplest, you'll wait for your cooked broth to cool a bit (but not too much, for health safety reasons), strain out (and discard) the solid materials, and get the broth cool enough (quickly enough) to place it in the refrigerator. Once it cools completely in the refrigerator, the fat will rise to the top.

Here are the steps to the process in more detail.

Harvesting Step 1: Turn Off the Appliance

When you're ready to harvest your bone broth, turn the appliance off (slow cooker, stove, oven, Sous Vide Supreme, or pressure cooker). Let it cool on the counter just enough so that you can handle it without burning yourself, but no longer. (It's important to get your broth into the refrigerator as quickly as possible, to prevent harmful bacteria from growing on it.)

Harvesting Step 2: Remove Bones and Other Material

Get a big bowl. Remove the bones using tongs and put them in the big bowl. Carefully scoop out any veggies and herbs, using a slotted spoon or spider strainer. You can add them to the bowl with the bones. Discard the bones and vegetables once they have cooled enough. DO NOT put hot bones into the garbage or they might melt the plastic trash bag, creating holes in it. I speak from experience here. There's nothing like lifting up a heavy garbage bag that melts into ribbons as you pick it up, dumping over-cooked vegetable mush, bones, and whatever else is in your garbage... all over the kitchen floor. Lesson learned: No hot bones in the trash!

Next, get another pot. Let's take a minute to talk about this pot, and why you shouldn't use a bowl. You'll be putting relatively hot broth into it, and then cooling it quickly in an ice bath. A metal bowl will get too hot to touch (I speak from experience). On the other hand, a glass or ceramic bowl can crack when subject to the temperature extremes of hot broth on the inside, and ice water on the outside. I speak from experience here, too. So use a good, sturdy pot with a handle for transferring your broth into.

Harvesting Step 3: Strain the Broth

Ok, so you've now wisely chosen a pot. Now, it's time to strain the bone broth. Nest a strainer in the pot. Better yet, line the strainer with cheesecloth. For highest quality results, spend money on a well-worth-it chinois to get super clear broth. A chinois ("sheen-wah") is a conical sieve with an extremely fine mesh. It makes broth so beautiful you'll wish there was a bone broth competition because you'd take home the blue ribbon. Note: Chinois are fairly large, so you'll need a large enough pot to accommodate it.

Pour the broth through the strainer and into the receiving pot. If you're strong, brave, and confident, you can do this by just lifting the cooking vessel (i.e., the slow cooker insert, the stock pot, the Dutch oven, the Sous Vide Supreme, or the pressure cooker), and pouring it. Caution! Be sure the cooking appliance isn't too hot to hold. Or too heavy! You can use oven mitts, if necessary. If the appliance is too hot or heavy to handle, then use a Pyrex glass measuring cup (or any ol' mug), and scoop the broth out of the cooking vessel – cup by cup – pouring it through the strainer and into the receiving pot.

Harvesting Step 4: Cool in an Ice Bath

Once strained, you want to cool your broth as quickly as possible, for food safety. It's ice bath time! An ice bath is equal parts ice and cold water. I typically use my sink, filling it with enough ice and water to submerge 3/4 of the pot. Sinks are nice because they're convenient to fill, drain, and they're large enough to accommodate any size pot I'm likely to use.

Prepare the sink with the ice bath and gently set the bowl of broth to cool inside it, taking care that the bowl doesn't tip from buoyancy and let any of the cold water spill into it. Occasionally stirring the broth with a spoon will speed the cooling process. Circulating the ice water outside the pot will also help speed the process. You may also want to drain some of the ice bath and add more water and ice if the water is no longer cold.

As an alternative (and being careful!), you can transfer the bone broth into glass mason jars and set those in the ice bath in the sink. I've even made ice baths using large rectangular plastic bins (coolers work, too). Again, you have to be careful here, and let the broth cool enough first! If the broth is too hot and you put the jar into the ice bath, it can crack the jar. Also, do not be tempted to sidestep this whole ice bath thing and just stick the hot mason jars in the freezer. They will crack. Trust me... it's very messy to clean multiple pints of frozen broth splashed all over the inside of your freezer the next day. (In my defense, I do the risky experiments so you don't have to!)

Or, do what my nana and my mom did while I was growing up in Michigan. During winter, when there was snow outside, my mom would take the stock pot full of broth and just cool the damn thing by setting it outside in the snow! She'd leave it there overnight. I love that.

Harvesting Step 5: Transfer the Broth into Jars

After a while, remove the pot from the ice bath and pat it dry with a towel. If the side of the pot is still warm, but not painful to touch, then you can now transfer the broth into jars (or other containers with lids).

Place the jars full of bone broth in the refrigerator for at least a few hours, or until you see the fat rise to the top. At this point, decide how much of the fat, if any, you want for the broth. If you decide to take some or all of it out, set it aside. Don't throw this fat away! It's a fantastic fat for roasting or sautéeing vegetables. My mom likes to freeze the fat in an ice cube tray and then just takes out what she needs from the freezer whenever she cooks vegetables.

If you're going to consume the bone broth within the next 5 days, simply keep the jars in the refrigerator, and consume as desired. If you want to freeze some or all of the broth to use later, you can put the containers in the freezer, but make sure they are only 3/4 full, or you risk breaking the glass jars or plastic seals as the broth freezes and expands.

Harvesting Step 5 (Optional): FoodSaver for Extra Freezer Space

If you're making a lot of broth, or if you make it routinely like I do, then you'll quickly run out of freezer space storing broth this way. Therefore, my favorite way to store the broth for freezing is to transfer it to freezer-safe zip bags or, even better, FoodSaver storage bags if you have a FoodSaver vacuum-seal device. This allows you to stack the flat bags and fit more in your freezer. Of course, you could always just buy an extra freezer if you have the space. I did that, and it came in handy when I was ordering an eighth of a cow at a time (for meat), plus boxes of bones and bags of chicken feet. The cost of the freezer paid for itself many times over by allowing me to purchase in bulk. (Though you might want to invest in a small backup generator if you live in an area with frequent power outages.)

The brilliance of the FoodSaver for storing bone broth is that it keeps it as fresh as possible while frozen, because nearly all of the air gets sucked out of it. If you have never FoodSavered liquids before, it's fairly simple, although it requires a bit of practice and balance to get a system down where you never spill a drop. Consider enlisting an extra set of hands to help.

If you're alone, or feeling feisty, you can instead do what I call my "FoodSaver Dance."

After gently pouring bone broth into a FoodSaver bag (taking care to not fill it too high), I use both hands to place the open edge of the bag on the FoodSaver while supporting the weight of the bag on my knee, while I stand on one leg. It's nuts, but it works. I hardly ever fall over spilling broth everywhere when doing this.

It's actually quite easy once you get the hang of it. I pinky-swear it. If you don't have a FoodSaver, no big deal. (Though I recommend getting one because they're awesome for saving food!) You can do a pretty decent job by simply using large, freezer-safe, Ziploc bags and manually pushing the air out before zipping it shut.

If you have an Amazon wish list, know that there exists an ultimate, high-end solution!: A device that specializes in vacuum-sealing liquids(!) called a "chamber vacuum sealer." Okay, so it's pretty expensive ($600-$1000, whatever), but it would make this whole process sooo much faster, easier, and James Bond-like. You might get so good and fast at making bone broth that you start giving it out for holidays and birthdays. Heck, maybe even start a hipster bone broth delivery business. If that's not enough to make you drop $600, my husband asked if he could modify it to use vapor deposition to grow synthetic diamonds. So there's that. Or just do the FoodSaver Dance and cancel your yoga studio membership.

Bone Broth Pucks

Lastly, while we're on the subject of freezing bone broth, recall that I freeze it in cute little silicone molds for my daughter as super nutritious, if socially awkward, snacks.

Well, there's an adult version. I've poured bone broth into silicone muffin trays (set on top of a baking tray so they don't spill due to their flexible nature - sigh, more experience speaking here). Then, I freeze it. Once frozen, these little bone broth pucks are easy transfer into Ziploc freezer bags for convenient, single-serving use. No need to thaw an entire jar or cut open a FoodSaver bag when all I want is a single mug of broth, or one portion to add to whatever I'm cooking for dinner.

Remember That Fat I Said to Save?

If you had set aside the fat, it's great to keep it around for a few days and cook with it. I dab off any wetness and transfer it to a container with an airtight lid and store it in the refrigerator for up to a week. Or, like my mom does, in the freezer for several months.

Chapter 7

BONE BROTH EQUIPMENT

Bone Broth Cooking Appliances

As I've mentioned earlier in this book, there are a number of ways you can cook bone broth:

- Slow cooker
- Stove
- Oven
- Pressure cooker
- Sous Vide Supreme

This chapter will go over each method in further detail. You will detect a pattern: The directions are nearly identical for each appliance. The only differences are for the cooking times and the amounts of broth that can be made. For this reason, you may wish to skip ahead to your preferred appliance, if you already know what it is. You won't miss anything important.

But first, a word about quantity.

Go Big or Go Home

It's best to get a large cooking vessel if you plan to make larger quantities, such as if you plan on making bone broth a regular staple in your diet – and I recommend that you do!

Getting the right equipment for making large batches will save you a TON of time. Big appliances also means you'll always be able to include anything your heart desires in your bone broth (hey there, beef knuckles!)

My first few batches as a bone broth newbie were cooked in a measly 6-quart slow cooker. Not big enough... I'd go through it in no time. So I quickly graduated to an 8-quart slow cooker, much better. I also have a large stock pot, an Instant Pot pressure cooker, and a Sous Vide Supreme (water oven).

I've made bone broth in all of them, many times. If I had to list my favorite ways to cook bone broth, it would be a tie between the Sous Vide Supreme and the pressure cooker (I prefer the Instant Pot for my electric pressure cooker).

They're very different though. I love the Sous Vide Supreme for it's precise temperature control and ability to make enormous batches (though you can use it for smaller batches, too). I love the Instant Pot because it's so convenient and quick.

That said, when I first started making bone broth and I used a slow cooker, that was great, too. It allowed me to make quantities larger than my Instant Pot (though you can buy larger 8-quart Instant Pot).

Regardless of which appliance you use, you'll essentially be doing the same thing: Put the bones and water in the cooking vessel and turn it on. The only difference is the time required for cooking. If you use a pot on a stove, a Sous Vide Supreme, or a slow cooker, then cooking chicken bone broth typically takes 6 to 12 hours (and up to 24, if desired). In these same appliances, cooking beef (or lamb or pork) bone broth optimally requires 24 to 48 hours.

Compare these times to the pressure cooker, where you can cook the exact same chicken for as little as 60 minutes! By the time the pressure cooker naturally releases the pressure, your bone broth might have taken a total of 2 hours or less to make. For beef or pork bones in a pressure cooker, I cook it for 90 minutes before letting the pressure come down naturally (usually another 30 to 45 minutes).

Lastly, there's fish. I only make fish bone broth in a pot on a stove because the cooking time needs to be short and gentle (less than an hour). It's also easy to keep an eye on a pot on the stove.

All of the above appliances are easy and you can't go wrong, whether you make it on the stove or in an appliance like a slow cooker, Sous Vide Supreme, or pressure cooker. Here are detailed instructions for each method.

Slow Cooker - Bone Broth Directions

I'll start with detailing how to make bone broth in a slow cooker. Though chefs and culinary enthusiasts prefer to make bone broth in a proper stock pot on the stove, a slow cooker is easier to manage. If you have a large slow cooker (8-quarts), I'd recommend starting here. If it's only a 6-quart slow cooker, start there for your first batch. Once you get the hang of it, I'm sure you'll want to upgrade to a larger one. This will allow larger batches and it'll free up the smaller slow cooker to cook other things.

Important: Roast the Bones

Before you start cooking your broth, it's time to get the bones roasted for the optimal flavor if you're making beef, lamb, or pork bone broth. (See the instructions in Chapter 6 for roasting bones.) If you're making chicken bone broth, you can optionally skip the roasting step. If you're making fish bone broth, don't roast the bones and don't use a slow cooker. Instead, use a soup pot on the stove.

While the bones are roasting, get your slow cooker out and fill it about half full with water. Add a splash of vinegar or wine, if desired. Once the bones are done roasting, add them to the slow cooker. Decide now if you want to add anything else, such as vegetables or seasoning (don't add salt). After you have added all the items you want in your slow cooker, add enough water to cover it all. Important: Do not fill your slow cooker too high, or it will bubble over.

Turn your slow cooker on LOW, put on the cover, and walk away. Cook 24 hours for chicken bone broth. Cook 24 to 48 hours for beef (or lamb or pork) bone broth.

During this time, you can open the lid occasionally and give it a quick stir. You might notice that some of the liquid has boiled off. You can add more water at this time, or not. It's up to you. Adding more water dilutes the broth, but it might be necessary if it hasn't cooked long enough and you want to extract more nutrition from the bones. Don't let it run out of water completely.

When the time is up, you're ready to harvest your broth (see Chapter 6).

Stock Pot on the Stove - Bone Broth Directions

In classic French cooking, you use a proper stock pot to cook bone broth, and it's cooked on the stove. The benefit of a stock pot is that it's designed to be taller than it is wide for proper evaporation. You also cook it without a lid. Stock pots come in many different sizes, so if you're looking to make big batches, there are big stock pots to do the job.

If you want to make classic stock (bone broth) like French chefs do, then I've provided the guidelines below. After that, it's pretty much the same as the other appliances, save a few minor appliance-specific differences. Although not classic cooking, I stand by my use of all kinds of unique ingredients in bone broth. While I use my bone broth in many other recipes, and simplicity can be essential there, I also drink it straight. By adding diverse ingredients, it can make drinking bone broth more exciting.

The basic elements and rules for stock, as recommended by classically trained chefs around the world, are as follows:

Ingredients:

- Bones and trimmings
- Mirepoix (in a ratio of 3 onion to 2 carrot to 1 celery). (Mirepoix is a sautéed mixture of diced vegetables used as a basis for soups, stews, and sauces.) The ratio of bones to mirepoix should be 2 part bones to 1 part mirepoix.
- Head of garlic (cut horizontally and thrown in)
- Bouquet garni (thyme, bay leaves, parsley, and small handful of peppercorns... dried thyme and bay leaves can be used).
- Optional: Tomatoes or tomato paste (for beef or veal stocks). If making chicken bone broth, do not use liver or tomato.
- NO SALT - Never salt your stock, because if you want to reduce it for a sauce later, you can't control the saltiness. This is another reason you don't want to use store bought stock for reducing into sauces. They're usually salted.
- Vinegar – The classic method doesn't use vinegar. However, many think the vinegar is helpful for extracting more nutrition from the bones. It's your choice.

Important: Roast the Bones

Before you start cooking your broth, it's time to get the bones roasted for the optimal flavor if you're making beef, lamb, or pork bone broth. (See the instructions in Chapter 6 for roasting bones.) If you're making chicken bone broth, you can optionally skip the roasting step. If you're making fish bone broth, don't roast the bones.

While the bones are roasting, get your stock pot and add some cold water to it, filling it about half way. Add a splash of vinegar or wine, if desired (more if it's a large stock pot). Once the bones are done roasting, add them to the stock pot. Decide now if you want to add anything else, such as vegetables or seasoning (don't add salt).

After you have the items you want in your stock pot, add enough water to cover the ingredients by 1 to 2 inches. Turn the stove on high and bring the mixture to barely a boil as quickly as possible, and then immediately turn it down to a simmer. Keep an eye on it, because chefs don't like their stock to boil! (Boiling makes the stock cloudy.)

Classically trained chefs use the following times for cooking stock:

- Chicken: 2 to 3 hours
- Beef/pork: 4 to 5 hours
- Veal: 10 to 12 hours
- Fish: 20 minutes

When the time is up, you're ready to harvest your broth (see Chapter 6).

Note: You may have noticed that I normally cook mine for longer than these times when using a slow cooker, as do most bone broth enthusiasts (yes, that's a thing). For us, most of the time we're trying to extract as much nutrition as possible; hence, the longer cooking times. If I cooked the bone broth on the stove for such extended times, I'd have my stove on all day and night, and I'd have to keep an eye on it regularly for evaporation. It's not practical or safe. This is why I rarely use a stock pot for cooking bone broth – it's not ideal for extracting maximum nutrition through long cooking times.

However, if I did use the stove, I'd follow the traditional French guidelines above for cooking times, just to make it safe and easy. I do like using the stove to make quicker batches of bone broth when making chicken bone broth, if I don't have my pressure cooker or slow cooker - like when I'm traveling. The reality is that anything is better than nothing, and there will still be plenty of flavor. So, if I cook the bone broth for only a few hours, so be it. When traveling, a stove and a pot are usually all that's available. I make do with what I have. (For fish, use the classic cooking guidelines and cook it less than an hour, on the stove.)

Dutch Oven in the Oven - Bone Broth Directions

You can use your Dutch oven (or similar oven-cooking pot with a lid), inside the oven, to make bone broth. When I opt for cooking bone broth in the oven, it's because I've roasted a chicken already in the Dutch oven, and I decide to return the carcass back to it (with any other scraps already in there), adding water, and cooking it. Again, the bigger the better for this. If your Dutch oven isn't very big then you won't make large quantities, but sometimes that's just fine. However, if you had enough bones (and two Dutch ovens), you could put both in the oven to cook bone broth. That would give you a bigger quantity, while only using the oven one time.

Making bone broth in the oven requires running your oven multiple hours in a day. Not ideal, but completely doable. As a result, you're unlikely to let the broth cook as long as you would in a slow cooker (or Sous Vide Supreme). The broth will still be tasty, but might not have enough time to extract all the nutrients.

Important: Roast the Bones

Before you start cooking your broth, it's time to get the bones roasted for the optimal flavor if you're making beef, lamb, or pork bone broth. (See the instructions in Chapter 6 for roasting bones.) If you're making chicken bone broth, you can optionally skip the roasting step. If you're making fish bone broth, don't roast the bones and don't use a Dutch oven; instead, use a soup pot on the stove.

While the bones are roasting, get your Dutch oven and fill it with water about half way. Add a splash of vinegar or wine, if desired. Once the bones are done roasting, add them to the Dutch oven. At this point, you need to decide if you want to add anything else such as vegetables or seasonings (don't add salt).

After you have the items you want in your Dutch oven, add enough water to cover it all. Do not to fill your Dutch oven too full or it could bubble over. Put the lid on. You can go low temperature and slow cooking time by setting the oven to about 200 degrees F, and let it cook for the day. Or you can raise it to 325 degrees F and let it cook for 5 to 7 hours. Check on the water level periodically. Add water if it's decreased too much, and continue cooking.

When you're ready to harvest your bone broth, turn the oven off and use pot holders or oven mitts to take the Dutch oven out of the oven. Take the lid off and let the Dutch oven cool until you can handle it. Finish the harvesting process by following the directions in Chapter 6.

Pressure Cooker - Bone Broth Directions (Using an Instant Pot)

I'm eager to share the process for making bone broth using Instant Pot Pressure Cooker, because it's one of my favorite ways! Using an Instant Pot to make bone broth is super easy... and super fast. I can cook it in just over an hour, due to the nature of the pressure cooking. My Instant Pot is 6-quarts, so I can't make large batches of bone broth with it, but I still love it. Instant Pot now makes an 8-quart version, which I'll buy the next time I'm in the market for a pressure cooker.

I can't speak to the level of nutrition in the bone broth when using an Instant Pot. It cooks for much less time. However, it's cooking under pressure, which means hotter – so, maybe it gets the same nutrition as a slow cooker, but in less time? I'm not sure. I'm confident there is at least some nutrition in it, even if it might not be as much as there is in a long, slow-cooked bone broth. The Instant Pot also might not make broth that's as clear and beautiful because of this high temperature cooking. I still love it. I get plenty of flavor, and I can make mini batches, which can actually be a welcome thing from time to time, or might be just right for singles, or if you're the only one in your family drinking bone broth.

The bottom line about making bone broth in pressure cookers: It greatly reduces cooking time, meaning there are simply more opportunities to make and consume broth. And that means getting more of it in your life.

Important: Roast the Bones

Before you start cooking your broth, it's time to get the bones roasted for the optimal flavor if you're making beef, lamb, or pork bone broth. (See the instructions in Chapter 6 for roasting bones.) If you're making chicken bone broth, you can optionally skip the roasting step. If you're making fish bone broth, don't roast the bones and don't use a pressure cooker; instead, use a soup pot on the stove.

While the bones are roasting, get out your Instant Pot. Once the bones are done roasting, add them to the Instant Pot. At this point, decide if you want to add anything else, such as vegetables or seasoning (do not add salt). Because the Instant Pot has limited room, I stick with just bones and water. Add enough water to fill the Instant Pot to the maximum level it specifies (follow the manufacturer's instructions for how much you can put in it before adding the lid). Add a splash of wine or vinegar if desired.

Secure the lid. Turn on your Instant Pot and choose "High Pressure." Select 60 minutes for chicken bones and 90 minutes for lamb, pork, or beef bones. When it's done cooking, let the pressure slow-release naturally. Remove the lid. You're now ready to harvest your broth (see Chapter 6).

Sous Vide Supreme - Bone Broth Directions

I've saved the best for last. Making bone broth with a Sous Vide Supreme quickly became my favorite method because I could make a lot, I could control the temperature carefully (resulting in extra beautiful broth), and it was super easy to use.

"Sous vide" (pronounced "soo veed") is a cooking method in which items are placed into a plastic bag, which is sealed and then submerged in a "water oven," in which the water is precisely regulated (and sometimes circulated, depending on the model). This method ensures a level of even, consistent cooking that can't be obtained using other methods available in the kitchen. For instance, in a sous vide you can't burn the food and it can't dry out, no matter how long you leave the food in it.

I bought my sous vide appliance, specifically a Sous Vide Supreme, shortly after we stopped eating a vegan diet. I was cooking steaks and without much success. I was always overcooking them. I had been vegan for so long that I actually didn't have any steak-cooking experience! My husband went online in search of help. He came across an article discussing the many merits of sous vide cooking, most notably the promise of perfectly cooked meat, every time.

I was immediately intrigued. If I could eat more meat and enjoy it at the same time, I was in! Interestingly, though, this amazing machine also takes the tough and cheap cuts of meat and makes them fork-tender. So, I bought one. And, it paid for itself when I could save money on the cuts of meat I was buying and the huge batches of broth I could make.

At the time, the Sous Vide Supreme was the only game in town, for consumers anyway. Today, you have choices, including "immersion" devises that don't include a large oven; rather, they submerge in one of your pots:

Sous Vide Supreme   Wancle Sous Vide Cooker

The sous vide was never intentionally designed for making bone broth. It just happened that, with the Sous Vide Supreme, you could, and it works great. The Sous Vide Supreme is a large, rectangular cooking appliance that you fill with water. If you're using the Sous Vide Supreme as it's designed, and making meat for example, you'd vacuum seal the meat. Then, you put the vacuum-sealed meat inside the Sous Vide Supreme (remember, it's filled with water). It's a complete unit where you cook the food inside it. Some call it a water bath for cooking. However, using this model for making bone broth does not involve vacuum sealing anything. Instead, you put the water, bones, and your ingredients right inside, as if it were a slow cooker or stock pot. The beauty is in being able to control the temperature to the exact degree you want.

The alternate submersion models of sous vide create the same conditions (water bath), but instead of a "water oven," you use your own pot to hold the water. You then clip the sous vide device on to the side of your pot to heat the water. So, you wouldn't use one of these newer versions where you stick the sous vide in your own pot because you'd be sticking the thing inside broth! But, with the Sous Vide Supreme, it's essentially an electric, finely-controlled-temperature cooking appliance where you won't damage it by cooking broth in it.

Funny thing is the Sous Vide Supreme is not advertised for making bone broth, although it should be. I never dreamed of having anything inside it other than water and the vacuum-sealed meats. However I was looking through a cooking website one day that specialized in sous vide cooking, and I saw them use it for bone broth. Brilliant!

The Sous Vide Supreme is an expensive appliance at first glance ($430). However, if you factor in the ease with which you can make bone broth, as well as the money you save cooking tough and cheap cuts of meat many times... well, the price isn't too bad. Plus, you'd have a Sous Vide Supreme, which will definitely be the talk of any parties you host. And you can use it for a lot more than just making broth! I love mine so much that I've even taken it on road trips to cook perfect steaks... in our hotel room. (A bit over the top, I admit.)

As I said, one of my favorite reasons for using a Sous Vide Supreme for cooking bone broth is because it allows complete control of the temperature. This means that it doesn't simmer too heavily or boil, which can happen in a slow cooker. It's also BIG and I can make huge batches of bone broth each time. That's a time saver.

Why is it important to maintain the temperature of your bone broth? Kitchen professionals will tell you that stocks should never boil, and some say it shouldn't even simmer, because it makes the stock "imperfect". Once stock (bone broth) simmers or boils, you get an end result that's "cloudy" in taste, feel, and look. I don't know what "cloudy" tastes like, but I do know that slow cookers are easy and cheap. I'm also the first to admit that sometimes perfection is over-rated. So, if simmering is how you want to make bone broth, then join the other millions of people through history who've simmered their stock and love every drop of it. The important thing is making it. And don't boil it. :)

However, if you fancy making huge batches of gorgeous bone broth that don't require a watchful eye, then the Sous Vide Supreme is THE answer. When you use a stock pot or slow cooker, the water evaporates, requiring that you check on it once in a while and add more water. The Sous Vide Supreme, however, has a lid that fits tight enough to prevent the evaporating water to escape (instead, it just drips back into the stock). This really makes the Sous Vide Supreme a largely hands-off operation.

Important: Roast the Bones

Before you start cooking your broth, it's time to get the bones roasted for the optimal flavor if you're making beef, lamb, or pork bone broth. (See the instructions in Chapter 6 for roasting bones.) If you're making chicken bone broth, you can optionally skip the roasting step. If you're making fish bone broth, don't roast the bones and don't use a sous vide; instead, use a soup pot on the stove.

While the bones are roasting, get out your Sous Vide Supreme and add some water to it, filling it about 1/2 to 2/3 full (you'll top it off with more water after you've added all of the ingredients). Add a few splashes of vinegar or wine, if desired. Once the bones are done roasting, add them to the Sous Vide Supreme. At this point, you need to decide if you want to add anything else such as vegetables or seasoning (don't add salt). After you have the items you want in your Sous Vide Supreme, add enough water to cover it all.

Turn on the Sous Vide Supreme and set the temperature to 194 degrees F. Put on the cover, and walk away. Watch Netflix for 24 to 48 hours for beef (or lamb or pork) bone broth and 12 to 24 hours for chicken bone broth. You can leave it alone the whole time (ahem, Netflix). When the time is up, you're ready to harvest your broth (see Chapter 6).

Chapter 8

EXTRA RECIPES

Bacon Egg Soup

Yield 1 serving

This is a great breakfast, lunch or dinner recipe. It's satisfying and warming. Kids like it, too!

- 2 cups bone broth
- 2 eggs, lightly whisked
- 2 to 4 strips of cooked bacon, chopped
- sea salt, to taste

1. Heat the broth on the stove to a simmer.
2. Slowly pour the eggs into the soup and stir to create a cooked ribbon of eggs.
3. Once the eggs are cooked to your liking, pour the soup into a big mug or a bowl.
4. Stir in the cooked bacon.
5. Taste and season with salt.

Longevity Bone Broth

Here's a bone broth full of longevity-boosting ingredients. For the amounts given below, I make it in a Sous Vide Supreme, but you can reduce the amounts to fit a stock pot or slow cooker.

- 7 oz fresh turmeric root, chopped
- 4 oz fresh ginger root, sliced
- 3 oz fresh lemongrass, bruised (mash down on it like a clove of garlic)
- 1/2 oz dried astragalus root
- 1 ounce kombu
- 4 to 5 pounds beef bones (a mix of knuckles and marrow bones)
- 1 to 2 pounds stew beef (optional)
- 2 carrots, halved
- 3 stalks celery, halved
- 1 red onion, halved
- 1/4 cup red wine

1. Roast the bones, stew beef, and onion in a large roasting pan at 350 degrees F for about 45 minutes (flipping the bones half way through the cooking time). Take the onions and beef out early if they look like they're charring too much.
2. Put all of the ingredients into the Sous Vide Supreme set to 194 degrees F.
3. Add enough water to cover.
4. Cook 24 to 36 hours.
5. Harvest the broth per the instructions in Chapter 6.

Bone Broth Reduced Sauce

One of the main reasons I love bone broth is what it does to my everyday cooking - taking meals to the next level. It makes healthy meals taste so much better from the extra meaty flavor it imparts.

One super delicious way to use bone broth is to make sauces by reducing the bone broth. This concentrates the flavor. And it's simple. Remember, this should be *unsalted* broth or don't even bother making a sauce with it, or it'll be reduced to a salt lick.

1. Place a small sauce pan on the stove.
2. Add 1 cup of bone broth.
3. Turn the heat to high and get the broth to barely a boil before lowering the heat to maintain a simmer.
4. Let it reduce to a viscosity that coats a spoon when you dip it in. Don't worry too much about the exact viscosity, as any reduction of broth will yield an amazing sauce, whether it's thick or thin. "Coating a spoon" is just a general guideline.
5. Season with salt and pepper for taste.

Dehydrated Broth Powder - A Brilliant Convenience

This is a great way to use your dehydrator, if you have one. The work involved is worth it, and most of the process is hands off. It just involves time, occasionally monitoring the bone broth while it's reducing. It always shocks me how little of the powder you get, once you reduce and dehydrate all that stock. But that's okay – it only takes a small amount of this amazing powder to make a delicious mug of bone broth.

The best part? Dehydrated bone broth stores very well, and at room temperature. No messing with the freezer or refrigerator. With frozen broth in jars, you have to make sure you thaw it before heating it up to drink it, and that can take days in the refrigerator. If it's frozen in bags, you still have to thaw it (though that's a bit easier in bags because you can put them in warm water). With bone broth powder, you just heat some water and stir the dehydrated bone broth into it. This is where the up-front "work" of dehydrating really pays off later. Your future self will thank you.

Dehydrated bone broth powder also makes it easy to enhance all of your meals with delicious, meaty flavors. Instead of, again, relying on the timing of having bone broth thawed and ready to use, you can add a bit of dehydrated bone broth to power up flavors and nutrition of meals. Add a spoonful to soups, stews, chili, grains, casseroles, etc.

Dehydrated bone broth also makes a perfect travel food! In fact, I think everyone should have dehydrated bone broth in their cupboard ready to take for travel on a moment's notice. Imagine going to the airport with this and then getting a cup of hot water once you're through security. You can sip delicious and nourishing bone broth, while sitting in the airport or on the plane!

Or, take it camping. Place bone broth powder in individual storage bags, along with pieces of dried vegetables, beef jerky, and a little salt (if desired). (Or, just keep it simple with bone broth powder.) Rehydrate with water over a campfire stove. There's nothing better than a nice, warm mug of broth when you're camping in chilly weather. This means you can have bone broth to drink that doesn't take up cooler space. You can also use it to season any foods you're making.

Dehydrated bone broth powder is also great for work. Keep a small jar of it at work without worrying about refrigeration. Now you can stay nourished and warmed, while at work, drinking this delicious elixir.

Directions:

1. Make your bone broth, as usual, per the instructions in Chapter 6.
2. Refrigerate the broth and scrape the solidified fat off the top once it has hardened. Remove as much as possible.
3. Put the broth in a large soup pot. Simmer it until it has reduced almost completely. It should be thick with a gravy-like consistency.
4. Drizzle the broth onto non-stick dehydrator sheets.
5. Set the dehydrator to the highest temperature and dehydrate

until it is dry. At this point, it should snap into pieces and it won't feel sticky.

6. Grind it to a powder in a coffee grinder, blender, or with a mortar and pestle. It doesn't have to be a fine powder, just do what you can.

7. To reconstitute, mix 1 cup of hot water with 1 to 2 teaspoons (depending on the size of the granules) of dehydrated bone broth.

15-Minute Bone Broth Pasta (in the Instant Pot)

Yield 4 to 6 servings

I love my Instant Pot because it drastically cuts the time I need to be in the kitchen making food. Here's how I use bone broth to make a ridiculously delicious, cheesy-meaty-pasta meal in 15 minutes with my Instant Pot.

- 2 to 4 tablespoons butter (I like lots of butter)
- 1 jar (25 oz or so) of your favorite marinara/pasta sauce
- sea salt, to taste (first note whether the pasta sauce is high in sodium)
- 1 box noodles (I like Jovial gluten-free)*
- 2 cups bone broth
- 1 pound ground beef, seasoned with salt
- mozzarella cheese, shredded or cubed

1. Put the butter, sauce, and salt in the Instant Pot.
2. Add the noodles.
3. Add the bone broth.
4. Add the ground beef on top of the noodles. (Break it into chunks or crumbles.)
5. Secure the lid. Set to LOW pressure for 5-minutes, or half the time listed on the box of pasta.*
6. When the time is up, quick release the pressure.

7. Add plenty of mozzarella. Stir it all together.

* Tip for cooking noodles in the Instant Pot, with respect to time and temperature: Cook them for HALF the time listed on the box and cook them on LOW pressure. Therefore, if my box reads 10-minutes, I'll cook on them on LOW for 5-minutes. If my box reads 9-minutes, then I'll round up and cook them for 5-minutes on LOW pressure.

Beef Roast with Bone Broth

Yield 4 to 8 servings

I make this recipe using an Instant Pot. (See below for slow cooker and Dutch oven variations.)

Instant Pot instructions:

- 1 (2 to 4 pounds) chuck roast, bone-in preferably
- sea salt and freshly ground black pepper
- 1 cup bone broth, unsalted

1. Decide whether you want to cook the roast whole, or in pieces. If you cut it in half, thirds, or big chunks, it'll cook faster. Generously season the meat with salt and pepper.
2. Pour the bone broth into the Instant Pot. Add the beef.
3. Secure the lid. Cook under HIGH pressure for 45 to 60 minutes. (Time will depend on the weight and size of the meat, as well as whether the meat was closer to room temperature before cooking or straight from the refrigerator. Experiment to find what time works best for you. Once you figure it out, write down the details for future use.)
4. Let the Instant Pot naturally release the pressure.
5. The beef should be so tender (for shredding) that it "trembles as the forks approach it." If it's not tender, cook under HIGH pressure for another 5 to 10 minutes, and try

again, with no need to naturally release pressure. You can quick release it at that point.

Slow Cooker Version

You can make this same recipe in a slow cooker or in a Dutch oven (on the stove).

For the slow cooker, put 2 to 3 cups of broth and seasoned meat into the slow cooker and cook on HIGH for up to 6 hours (until tender) or cook on LOW for up to 8 hours (until tender). Time varies based on the weight of the beef, the temperature of the beef when you put it into the slow cooker (room temperature is best), and whether it's been cut into chunks.

Dutch Oven Version

Place the ingredients into the Dutch oven and set it on the stove over medium-low heat. Cover the Dutch oven. You want a light simmer. Cook for 2 to 4 hours and check on it multiple times through the cooking to see if more broth is needed. Test for tenderness – the beef should fall apart easily. If it doesn't, it needs to cook longer. Time varies based on the weight of the beef and whether it's been cut into chunks.

Buttered Kale 'n' Broth

Yield 2 servings

Using the Instant Pot (pressure cooker) and some bone broth, you can quickly turn kale into something that actually tastes pretty good. (See below for directions on how to make this in a skillet.)

- 1 cup bone broth
- 1 bunch kale, chopped (or chard or collards)
- 1 to 2 tablespoons butter

- Sea salt and freshly ground black pepper, to taste
- 2 fried eggs, optional

1. Place the bone broth, kale, and butter in the Instant Pot. Secure the lid.
2. Cook under LOW pressure for 3 minutes.
3. Quick release the pressure when it's done cooking.
4. Divide the mixture between two bowls. Season with salt and pepper.
5. If you opted for fried eggs, top each bowl with one. Serve.

Skillet Directions

Place the bone broth, kale, and butter in a skillet and cook over medium-high heat until the kale is wilted and bright green. Season with salt and pepper. Serve. (Optional: Top with fried eggs.)

Bone Broth Beverages

Yield one serving each

It's time to have some groovy fun with bone broth. It can be used to make a variety of unique recipes, like the ones below. For all of these recipes, make sure you have a blender that can safely handle hot beverages. If you have a lid on your blender that doesn't allow steam to vent, the lid will blow off and you risk getting hot broth all over you, the floor, and the ceiling. If you don't have a proper blender for this, then consider hand whisking the ingredients or using an electric whisk. Both of these options work surprisingly well. It won't get as frothy as a high-powered blender, but it's still pretty damn good!

Another recommendation, though optional, is using broth that is extra strong in flavor. You can do this by reducing the bone broth before using it in the recipes. The strong flavors hold up to the butter and other additions. Furthermore, beef bone broth is a great choice, due to its rich, meaty flavor. However, a good strong chicken (or turkey) bone broth is amazing, too, especially for the Pumpkin Pie Broth recipe, below.

Buttered Bone Broth

- 1 to 2 cups of hot bone broth
- 1 to 2 tablespoons butter
- Sea salt, to taste

Blend the ingredients together until creamy and frothy (about 30 seconds).

Bacon Buttered Bone Broth

- 1 to 2 cups of hot bone broth (preferably pork bone broth)
- 1 tablespoon butter
- 1 to 2 teaspoons bacon fat
- Sea salt, to taste (probably not necessary if the bacon fat is salty)

Blend the ingredients together until creamy and frothy (about 30 seconds).

MCT Oil Brain-Powered Bone Broth

This recipe is in honor of Dave Asprey, for turning the world on to mixing butter with MCT oil in coffee.

- 1 to 2 cups of hot bone broth
- 1 tablespoon butter
- 1 tablespoon MCT oil
- Sea salt, to taste

Blend the ingredients together until creamy and frothy (about 30 seconds).

Bone Broth with Coconut Oil

- 1 to 2 cups of hot bone broth
- 1 tablespoon butter
- 1 tablespoon coconut oil
- Sea salt, to taste

Blend the ingredients together until creamy and frothy (about 30 seconds).

Mole Creamy Bone Broth

- 1 to 2 cups of hot beef bone broth
- 1 to 2 tablespoons butter
- 1/2 to 1 teaspoon cocoa powder
- 1 dash ground cinnamon
- 1 pinch cayenne powder
- Sea salt, to taste

Blend the ingredients together until creamy and frothy (about 30 seconds).

Golden Bone Broth

- 1 to 2 cups of hot bone broth
- 1 to 2 tablespoons butter
- 1/2 to 1 teaspoon ground turmeric powder
- 1/4 to 1/2 teaspoon ground ginger powder
- Sea salt, to taste

Blend the ingredients together until creamy and frothy (about 30 seconds).

Pumpkin Pie Bone Broth

- 1 to 2 cups of hot chicken or turkey bone broth
- 2 tablespoons pumpkin puree
- 1 to 2 tablespoons butter
- 1/4 to 1/2 teaspoon ground pumpkin spice powder
- Sea salt, to taste

Blend the ingredients together until creamy and frothy (about 30 seconds).

Have fun and experiment with different options and spices.

Simple Sunday Chicken Bone Broth (Instant Pot Recipe)

Yield 1 to 2 quarts

There's no excuse for buying chicken broth when you can make your own effortlessly. After enjoying a whole chicken that you cooked for the family, don't throw those bones out! They're packed with deliciousness and super nutrition! Want it even more nutritious? Add chicken feet!

- Chicken bones, raw or previously roasted
- Water
- 1 bay leaf, optional
- Splash of vinegar or wine, optional

1. Place the chicken bones into the Instant Pot and add a few cups of water. I like to add enough to almost cover the bones. Keep in mind, with a pressure cooker, you should never fill it

to the top, so be mindful to fill it to the designated line inside the Instant Pot.

2. Add the bay leaf and vinegar or wine.
3. Secure the lid. Cook on HIGH pressure for 60 minutes. Once it's done cooking under pressure, let it naturally release. Then, remove the lid.
4. Follow harvesting directions in Chapter 6.

If you want to make beef, lamb, or pork bone broth, you follow the exact same instructions as above, but you cook it under high pressure for 90 minutes and then let it naturally release. For beef or pork bones, remember to roast them first, per the instructions in Chapter 6. Then, follow the same instructions for harvesting in Chapter 6.

CONCLUSION & FREE PDF

As you can see, bone broth is very easy to make and can be a powerful addition to your diet, if you drink it on a regular basis.

For longevity, healthy skin, healthy joints, and more, I hope the information in this book has inspired you to make bone broth a regular fixture in your life. And, really there are no excuses, right? With so many ways to make it, from different appliances to different bones, you're sure to find a method and recipe that you love. And, even if you only drink it on occasion, it's a nourishing and delicious beverage that can warm your heart, body, and soul.

I'd love to hear from you and how your experience with bone broth is going. Perhaps I can add your story to a future edition of the book! Please keep in touch via twitter (http://Twitter.com/KristensRaw) or email (Kristen@GlobalKristen.com).

Free PDF

For a free, printable .PDF "Bone Broth Cheat Sheet" (which includes the recipes in this book), email me at kristen@globalkristen.com.

Did you enjoy this book? If so, please leave a review!

As an independent author, your reviews are extremely helpful in getting the word out. After you leave a review, please drop me a line at kristen@globalkristen.com so I can thank you!

Other books by Kristen Suzanne

The Carnivore Diet Handbook

The Frugal Carnivore Diet

Carnivore Diet Intermittent Fasting

Sardine Solution

Recipes with Sardines

∼

Kristen's blog at: GlobalKristen.com

Twitter: @KristensRaw

Instagram: global_kristen

Made in the USA
Coppell, TX
21 December 2020

46437542R00056